A Complete Guide To The Art Of Shorthand Writing

TO THE LEARNER.

BEFORE entering upon the exercises of this interesting study, the Author wishes the Student to peruse attentively, the following lines on " Application" from the pen of the late Rev. Samuel Davenport, of Horsley, Derbyshire.

" It is incredible how much may be done by diligence and assiduity. The present state of the world, enlightened by arts and sciences, is a living proof, that difficulties, seemingly insuperable, and undertakings imagined to be impossible, may be accomplished. This consideration ought to be no mean spur to industry and application. We are not acquainted with the strength of our own minds, till we exercise them, nor to what length our abilities will carry us, till we put them to the trial. Men who want resolution, often desist from enterprises, when they have more than half effected

B

their purpose :—They are discouraged by difficulties and disappointments, which ought rather to excite their ardour, and redouble the vigour of their efforts to succeed.   Let any one consider with attention the structure of a common engine to raise water. Let him observe the intricacy of the machinery, and behold in what vast quantities one of the heaviest elements is forced out of its course ; and then reflect how many experiments must have been tried in vain, how many obstacles must have been overcome, before a frame of such wonderful variety in its parts, could have been put together ; after which, let him pursue his own enterprises, not without hopes of success in the end, while he supports the spirit of industry by considering how much m ay be done by patience and ingenuity."

The student must not be too anxious to write expeditiously at first, or he will be sure to make " more haste than good speed." Let his first aim be to execute the characters with *neatness* and *accuracy*, and expedition cannot fail to ensue.   To acquire proficiency, he must not content himself with merely *writing* all he is requested to do, but in executing his task, he should constantly refer to the original copy for imitation; the neglect of this, frequently causes the latter part to be performed much worse than the first.

MATERIALS FOR WRITING.

A good pencil is recommended as much the best to write with until the Learner is considerably advanced: when he may wish to preserve a copy of any miscellaneous subject in Short-Hand manuscript, it will be preferable to write with a pen.

CHOICE OF PENCILS.

In using pencils for writing, good ones may be considered the cheapest; common pencils being generally found either so hard and full of grit as to cut the paper, and render it unfit for use on the contrary side, or so soft as constantly to require cutting, which is no small impediment to quick writing. With a good pencil the above difficulties are entirely obviated, and the points are much less liable to break than those of an inferior kind. The drawing pencils

manufactured by Mr. Banks, of Keswick, in
Cumberland, marked H. H. may be recommended as being of an excellent quality, and
a proper degree of hardness for Short-Hand
Writing.   .

CHOICE OF PENS.

For writing Short-Hand, an elastic steel
pen, with a fine point, will be found to possess decided advantages over those made
from the common quill. That manufactured
by Mr. John Skinner of Sheffield, called the
"*Ne plus ultra*" steel pen, is strongly recommended, as its elasticity may be increased
or diminished at pleasure : but as the manu-
facturers of this article are constantly bring-
ing forward *something new*, the writer will
of course make his own selection.

CHOICE OF PAPER.

For every purpose of Short-Hand Writing,
Paper of a good quality, with a very smooth
surface, ought to be selected; so that the
pen or pencil may move with perfect free-
dom, and at the same time form the characters with neatness and perspicuity. As it is
impossible in using common rough paper, to

retain a fine point to any pencil, the characters are unavoidably made very large and
thick, thereby not only impeding the process
of expeditious writing, but establishing an
injurious practice of forming the characters
with carelessness; a habit which soon becomes too fully confirmed to be easily eradi-
cated.

DIRECTIONS FOR HOLDING PEN OR PENCIL.

As it is necessary to hold the pen much
more erect than is usual in common writing,
it will be found advisable to place the long
finger within three quarters of an inch from
the point, and the end of the thumb opposite
that of the forefinger. By attending to the
foregoing observations, the pen may be
moved in any direction with equal ease and
facility.

OF THE CONSONANTS.

The next thing to which the attention of
the Learner is directed, is that of becoming
perfectly familiar with the various characters
by which the consonants admitted in the

present system of Stenography, are respectively represented.

The most easy and expeditious mode of accomplishing this, is by writing the characters very frequently, in the same order as exhibited in the first and second exercises; imitating them as nearly as possible, in *size, form,* and *position,* and at the same time impressing upon the memory the name of each, by repeating the letter which it is intended to express.

EXERCISE I.

EXERCISE II.

EXERCISE III.

No.	Word				No.	Word			
1	b l s				29	p r t			
2	b n d				30	p l n			
3	b n g				31	p n g			
4	d s k				32	r s t			
5	d m p				33	r n d			
6	d r k				34	r f l			
7	f n g				35	s m r			
8	f s t				36	s n g			
9	f r m				37	s t k			
10	f l t				38	t r n			
11	g v n				39	t n g			
12	g m n				40	t s k			
13	g l d				41	v l m			
14	j m p				42	v x n			
15	j g r				43	v m p			
16	k n g				44	v r g			
17	k r l				45	w s p			
18	k m n				46	w n g			
19	k s t				47	x m t			
20	l n g				48	x p l			
21	l r k				49	x l t			
22	l m p				50	x t l			
23	m k r				51	y s t			
24	m s k				52	y n g			
25	m n r				53	y l d			
26	n m l				54	z f r			
27	n v r				55	z s t			
28	n g r				56	z n k			

B 5

EXERCISE III.   Continued.

#	word					#	word				
57	bndr					85	prnt				
58	brst					86	pstm				
59	dfnd					87	qstn				
60	dspr					88	qvrs				
61	dvrg					89	rndr				
62	fngr					90	rmbl				
63	frnd					91	rnsm				
64	frgv					92	srtn				
65	fstl					93	sngl				
66	gntl					94	stnd				
67	grnt					95	trgt				
68	grsp					96	tndr				
69	hlpr					97	trmp				
70	hndl					98	vrbl				
71	hrkn					99	vrmn				
72	hngr					100	vstl				
73	jrnl					101	vrgn				
74	jngl					102	wndr				
75	kstm					103	wlkm				
76	kndl					104	wngs				
77	kptn					105	wrks				
78	kvrn					106	xprs				
79	lftr					107	xtnd				
80	lmbr					108	xpln				
81	mngl					109	xmnd				
82	mstk					110	yngr				
83	nmrl					111	ylds				
84	nrvs					112	zfrs				

EXERCISE IV.

TO BE EXPRESSED IN SHORT-HAND CHARACTERS, IN THE SAME MANNER AS THAT OF THE PRECEDING.

1	b n k	26	p r s	51	b r n g	76	p l n t
2	b r l	27	p n l	52	b n g l	77	p r s n
3	b s t	28	q r t	53	b l n k	78	q l t d
4	d m n	29	q k n	54	d n g r	79	q r t r
5	d n r	30	q l t	55	d p r t	80	q n t m
6	d r g	31	r s k	56	f r s t	81	r n d m
7	f k l	32	r f t	57	f n t m	82	r s t k
8	f r k	33	s n k	58	f s t v	83	r m p l
9	g f t	34	s p l	59	g s p l	84	s l k n
10	g v r	35	s f t	60	g r n d	85	s n g l
11	h n g	36	t k n	61	h n t r	86	t m t d
12	h r k	37	t n l	62	h r m t	87	t r s t
13	h v n	38	v g r	63	h n d r	88	t m p l
14	j l t	39	v s l	64	j s t s	89	v l v t
15	j r k	40	v n t	65	j m b l	90	v k t m
16	k p l	41	w f t	66	k p t v	91	w n t r
17	k n d	42	w n k	67	k v r n	92	w s d m
18	k s l	43	w r n	68	k r m p	93	w f t d
19	l r g	44	x p l	69	l n g r	94	x p r t
20	l n k	45	x s t	70	l s t n	95	x s t d
21	l s t	46	x m n	71	m r t l	96	x p n s
22	m r k	47	y l p	72	m s t r	97	y d k n
23	m n d	48	y r d	73	m m b r	98	y r d s
24	n k l	49	z m r	74	u p k n	99	z n k l
25	n t k	50	z r l	75	n m b r	100	z n t k

ON JOINING THE CONSONANTS.

When the Learner has become so far acquainted with the Stenographic characters introduced in the preceding exercises, as to be able to write them with ease and expedition, he may begin to learn the method of joining them together, in the neatest possible manner.

In joining Short-Hand characters together, the first letter is *generally* made, as if no other was to be written, and the next (without lifting the pen) from the last point of the first, as if it had not been there; for instance, in order to join the letters, *b*, *s*, *t*, together, first make the semicircle for *b*, ⊂ , then, without taking off the pen, draw down the *s* from the last point of the *b*, thus, ⌐ , *bs*, to which add the short horizontal line for *t*, thus, ⌐ *bst*; and so on in like manner with nearly all the rest. All unnecessary angles must be avoided; one letter being made to run into another as much as possible; for instance where two reverse semicircles occur together, neither of them is to be made complete, but a small portion must be cut off each, as in the following examples ; ∿ *mn,* ∾ *nm,* ∫ *bl,* ∫ *lb,* &c. In the same manner, all letters lose a portion when preceding any character which commences with a loop; as for example, *nv* is not to be written thus, ⌒ but ⌒; *sk* not ⌒, but ⌒ ; by which means, a great saving of time is effected, and a general uniformity is preserved in the writing. The curved part of the character representing *r,* is omitted when joined with other letters ; making a simple oblique line, thus ∕ , the same as *d,* with this exception, *d* is always made *down* from right to left ; but *r* must in all cases be made *up* from left to right, as in the following examples, ⌒ *drk,* ⌒ *rndr,* &c.

EXERCISE V.

1	bl		29	bls	
2	bs		30	dwl	
3	fx.........		31	gld	
4	gt		32	grt	
5	gv.........		33	hlp	
6	hm		34	jst	
7	hs		35	kng......	
8	jt...... ..		36	lnd	
9	kp		37	sml	
10	km		38	sng	
11	kt		39	trn	
12	lb.........		40	txt	
13	mf.........		41	wnt	
14	mk		42	xtl	
15	mn		43	yng......	
16	nm		44	zfr	
17	nf.........		45	bnfts ...	
18	nv		46	dprt......	
19	pk........		47	dstrs ...	
20	pr		48	frgt	
21	pt		49	frwl	
22	rk		50	grnd......	
23	rx		51	hnds......	
24	sx		52	kndl......	
25	st		53	trnd......	
26	tk		54	trst	
27	ts..........		55	tndr	
28	yt		56	xlnt......	

MODE OF SPELLING.

In writing Short-Hand no particular regard need be paid to the usual method of spelling. The Learner must use such letters only, as he may consider indispensably necessary to give the sound of the word intended to be expressed. All silent letters should be omitted, and one letter frequently substituted for another. As examples in spelling will doubtless be more readily understood than numerous rules and exceptions, upwards of 300 have been selected and arranged in the Sixth, Seventh, and Ninth Exercises, embracing the various combinations of letters, to which are annexed, the word or words they may possibly express.

The following extract of a letter from Major Jack Downing, to his old friend Mr. Dwight, of the New York Advertiser, though rather a singular production, will serve to illustrate the reasons for deviating from the general mode of spelling.

" I only wish I had gone to school a leetle more when I was a boy—if I had, my letters now would make folks crawl all over: but if I had been to school all my lifetime, I know I never could be able to write more honestly than I have.   I am sometimes puzzled most plaguily to git words to tell jest exactly what I think, and what I know: and when I git'em I don't know exactly how to spell'em—but so long as I git the sound, I'll let other folks git the sense on't—pretty much as our old friend down to Salem, who bilt a big ship to go to China—he call'd her the '*Asha.*'   Now there is sich a thing as folks knowin too much; all the larned ones was puzzled to know who '*Asha*' was; and they never would know to this day what it ment, if the owner of the ship had'nt tell'd 'em that China was in '*Asha.*'   'Oh! ah!' says the larned folks, 'we see now—but that ain't the way to spell it.'   'What,' says he, 'if *A-s-h-a* don't spell *Asha*, what on earth does it spell?' And that stump'd 'em."

EXPOSITION OF THE CONSONANTS.

B.

B is represented in the present system of Stenography, by a small semicircle, thus ⟨ , (the reverse of *l* ⟩) always commencing at the top; as for example ⟨ *bsk,* ⟨⟨⟨ *brng, &c.*

B may be omitted in such words as *comb, dumb, tomb, &c.*

To express *bb,* the character for *b* must be made twice without lifting the pen, thus ⟨ . *Be,* forming a distinct syllable at the beginning of a word, is expressed by making the character for *b* twice its usual size; thus ⟨ writing ⟨⟨ *be-gt* for *begat, beget,* and *begot;* ⟨⟨ *be-km,* for *became* and *become, &c.*

C.

As the letter *c* has always the sound of either *k* or *s,* as heard in *calm, cap, cost, cup, certain, cent, celestial, &c.,* no distinct character has been assigned to represent it. See exposition of *k* and *s,* which must be substituted for *c,* according to its hard or soft sound.

For the expression of *ch,* when occurring together, see exposition of the double consonants in a subsequent page of this treatise.

D.

D is represented by a short oblique line, thus, ╱ (the reverse of *p* ╲) in all cases commencing at the top. Examples, ⤴ *dfr,* ⤸ *drk, &c.*

D at the end of a word, has frequently the sound of *t,* which letter may be substituted for the former, when more conveniently joined with the preceding character; writing *blst* for *blessed; xprst* for *expressed, &c.*

D may be omitted in such words as *friendship, landlord, landscape, &c.*

Dd, must be expressed by making the character for *d* twice separately, thus ⁄⁄, as ⁄⁄ *dd-n* for *deaden;* ⤳⁄ *kn-dd* for *candid, &c.*

F.

F is represented by two distinct characters, each composed of a small loop and horizontal line, thus, ͻ or ͻ ; either of which may be used according as it is found to combine most easily with the preceding character. Examples ⸝— *rft* ⸝—, *sft*, &c.

F must always be substituted for *gh* and *ph*, in such words as *cough, laugh, rough, tough, phantom, pheasant, philosopher,* &c.

Ff may be expressed thus ͻ–ͻ– or ͻͻ .

G.

G is represented by a small descending curve and horizontal line, thus ⌐ (the reverse of *j* ⌐) as in ⸜ *gd*, ⌐⌐ *grnt*, &c.

G and *gh* being silent, may be omitted in such words as *gnat, phlegm, feign, reign, resign, light, sight,* &c.

Gh occurring together in the middle or at the end of a word, have generally the sound of *f*, as heard in *enough, laugh, trough,* &c., and must be substituted by that letter accordingly.

Gg must be expressed thus ⸗⸗ , as in the word *gig,* &c.

H.

Two distinct characters have been appropriated to represent this letter, not only to render it more convenient in combination, but to afford a ready means of expressing the *present* and *past* tenses of the auxiliary verb *to have.**

Each of the characters representing *h* is composed of a large semicircle, the first being made twice the size of *m* ⌢, thus ⌢, the second twice that of *n* ⌣, thus ⌣, leaving the writer at liberty to use that which most easily combines with the preceding or following character. Examples, ⌣ *hāt*, ⌣ *hēr*, ⌣ *hī*, ⌢ *hŏp*, &c.†

Although *h* is silent at the beginning of some words, it will be preferable to use it in spelling, instead of the vowel which it may

---

* See exercise on the combination of the verbs.

† When the letter *h* is combined with a consonant in spelling any word, it is immaterial which character is used, but several of the vowels have here been unavoidably introduced, in order to illustrate in as simple a manner as possible, *how* and *when* these characters should be respectively applied.

happen to precede, writing *hrb* for *herb,*
instead of *ĕrb ; hnr* for *honour,* instead of
ŏnr, &c.

J.

J, which has a perfect uniformity of
sound, (except in hallelujah) is represented
by a small ascending curve and horizontal
line, thus ⌒, (the reverse of *g* ⌒) as in ⌐
jst, &c.

When *g* has a soft sound, *j* may be substituted for it, as in the words *gem, gin,
ginger, gipsey, &c.*

K.

K is also represented by two distinct characters, thus ⌒, and ⌣ ; either of which
must be used (as in the cases of *f* and *v,*)
according to its ready combination with ad-
joining letters. Examples, ⌐ *pk,* ⌒ *znk, &c.*

C and *ch* hard, as heard in *calm, cap, cast,
cup, chaos, chasm, chameleon, &c.,* must
always be expressed by this letter, as ⌒
kŏrd, for *chord* and *cord;* ⌐ *kn-dl,* for *can-
dle* and *kindle, &c.*

K may be omitted when preceding *n* in the same syllable, in such words as k*nave*, k*nee*, k*nock*, &c. *Kk* may be expressed thus ᢐ or ꞷ .

L.

L is represented by a small semicircle, thus ⟩ , (the reverse. of *b* ⟨) always commencing at the top. Examples, ꝺ— *lv*, ꝺ— *lng*, &c.

L being silent, may be omitted in such words as *cälf, cälm, pälm, sälve, tälk, wälk*, &c.

Ll must be expressed thus ⟩ , as in ⋁ꝫ *pr-l-l*, for *parallel*, &c.

M.

M is represented by a small semicircle, thus ⌒, (the reverse of *n* ⌣) as in ⤳ *mnd*, ⤳ *mrk*, &c.

Mm is expressed thus ⌢, as ⌢ᷱ *mmbr*, for *member*, &c.

N.

N is represented by a small semicircle,

thus ∪, (the reverse of *m* ∩) as in ⌣ *ntr*, ⌣ *nvr*, &c. *N* may be omitted at the end of such words as *kil*n *hym*n, *autum*n, *solem*n, &c.

Nn is expressed thus ⌣, as ⌣ *ln-n*, for *linen*, ⌣ *kn-n* for *cannon*, &c.

P.

P is represented by a short oblique line, drawn downwards from left to right, thus ╲ (the reverse of *d* ╱) as in ⌣ *pnt*, ⌣ *prt*, &c.

To express *pp*, the character for *p*, is made twice, thus. ╲╲ Examples, ⌣ *p-pl* for *people*, &c.

P may always be omitted in such words as *p*neumatics, *p*salm, *p*tisan, temp*t*, contemp*t*, cor*p*s, ras*p*berry, recei*p*t, &c.

Ph, except when silent, must be substituted by the letters *f* or *v*; as in the words *Nephew, Phebe, Stephen,* &c.

Q.

Q is represented by a small curve and perpendicular line, thus ⌐ (the reverse of *wh* ⌐) as in ⌣ *qk*, ⌣ *qrl*, &c.

Qu may be substituted by *k* in such words as *conquer, liquor, marque, risque, &c.*

Cu, frequently sound like *q,* and may be expressed by the same character; writing *qr* for *cure; se-qr* for *secure; l-o-q-tion* for *elocution, &c.*

R.

R, when joined with other letters, is represented by a short oblique line, thus ╱, always commencing at the bottom, as in ╱ *rst,* ╱ *rndr, &c.* (See page 37.)

R, when standing alone, denotes the words *are, art,* and *or,* and is expressed thus ╱, in all cases commencing at the curve.

Re, forming a distinct syllable at the beginning of a word, is also expressed by the curved *r,* as in ╱ *re-fer,* ╱ *re-gard, &c.*

To express *rr,* first make the simple oblique line, up thus ╱, then join the curved *r* to the last point of the former; thus ╱. Ex. ╱ *t-r-r* for *terror, &c.* *Rr* may also be expressed by making the simple oblique line twice, as in ╱ *tr-rnt,* for *torrent, &c.*

S.

S is represented by a short perpendicular line, thus | , always commencing at the top, as in ⌐ *sml*, ∪ *sng*, &c.

S, when silent, may be omitted, as in the words *corps, demesne, isle, island, puisne, viscount,* &c.

S has frequently the sound of *sh*, and must in such cases be substituted by the latter; writing *Asha*, for *Asia ; Prsha*, for *Persia*, &c.

A distinct character is assigned to represent the letters *sh* when occurring together, for which, see exposition of the double consonants.

Ss may be expressed by making the character for *s* twice separately, thus ‖, or by drawing one twice its usual length, thus | , as ⌐ or ⌐ *re-ss*, for *recess*, &c.

T.

T is represented by a short horizontal line, thus —, in all cases to be made from left to right. Ex. ⌐ *trn*, ⌐ *tndr*, &c.

c

T may be omitted in such words as *bustle, chasten, eclat, hautboy, mortgage,* &c.

Tt is expressed thus =, as ⅁ *tt-l,* for *tattle,* &c.

Th occurring together, is expressed by drawing the horizontal line for *t* twice its usual length, thus ——, as in ——⌒ *thm,* ——╱ *thr,* &c. See exposition of the Double Consonants.

V.

V is represented by two distinct characters, each composed of a *large* loop and horizontal line, thus ᠊ and ᠊ ;* leaving the writer at liberty to use either one or the other, as convenience in combination may require. Ex. ᠊ *lv,* ᠊ *nvr,* &c.

Vv may be expressed thus, ᠊ or ᠊ .

W.

Two distinct characters have been appropriated to represent the above letter, each composed of a small loop and large semicircle, thus ⌒ and ᠊, being twice the size

* The loops of the above characters are twice the size of those for *f.*

of *k*. Ex. ✑ *wā*, ✑ *wō*, ✑ *dwl*, ✑ *frwl*, &c.

W may be omitted in such words as *wrap*, *wreck*, *wretch*, *answer*, *sword*, &c.

For the expression of *wh*, see exposition of the Double Consonants.

X.

X is also represented by two distinct characters, each composed of a small curve and oblique line, thus ⟍ and ⟍ ; using that which most easily combines with the preceding letter. Ex. ⟨ *sx*, ⟍ *txt* ,&c.

X has the sound of *z*, at the beginning of proper names, as heard in *Xanthus*, *Xenophon*, *Xerxes*, &c., and must be substituted by that letter accordingly.

X may generally be substituted for *cks*, or *cts*, at the end of a word; writing ⟍ *fx* for *facts, fix*, and *fox*; ⋀ *rx* for *rocks* and *wrecks*, &c.

Y.

Y, when a consonant, as in *ye, your, yes, youth*, &c., is represented thus ⟩, (the reverse of *z* ⌒,) always commencing at the curve, as in ∠ *yt,* ⌒— *yng,* &c.

Y must always be substituted for *i*, in the final syllable of such words as *billiards, collier, million, onion, pinion, pannier,* &c.

Z.

Z is represented by a small curve and oblique line, thus ⌒ (the reverse of *y* ⌐,) in all cases commencing at the top. Ex. ⌒ *zfr,* ⌐ *znk,* &c.

Z may frequently be substituted for *s*, when it has the hard hissing sound of the former.

EXPOSITION OF THE DOUBLE CONSONANTS.

Ch.

When *c* and *h* occur together, and have the sound of *tsh*, as heard in *charm, chapter, chip, chosen, church,* &c., they must be represented thus ∕, always commencing at the curve. Ex. ⌒ *chl* for *chill,* ⌒— *chng,* for *change*; ∿ *chp-tr,* for *chapter,* &c.

Ch having a hard sound like *k*, as in *chaos, chorus, chymist,* &c., must always be

substituted by it; writing *skēm* for *scheme,*
skóól for *school,* &c.

Ch must be expressed by *sh,* in such
words as *chagrin, chaise, chamade, chande-*
lier, &c.

Sh.

Sh is represented thus ⟍ and ╱; the
first being an oblique line twice the length
of *p,* always commencing at the top, as in
⋎ *sho,* ⟍⊸ *shrt,* &c.; the second is an
oblique line twice the length of *d,* and may
be made either by an ascending or descending movement, as convenience of combination
may require. Ex. ⟋ *psh,* ⟋ *shtr,* &c.

Th.

Th is represented by a horizontal line
twice the length of *t,* thus ——; always
commencing at the left. Ex. ——⸝ *thā,* ——⸜
thō, ——⸝ *thnks,* &c.

Wh.

Wh, when occurring together, is represented thus ⌠, (the reverse of *q* ⌐,) as in
the following examples. ⌐ *whn,* ⌐ *whr,*
⌐ *wht,* &c.

EXERCISE VI.

With a view to facilitate the progress of the Learner, as much as possible in reading Short Hand manuscript; the word or words which each example may denote have been placed immediately at the right of the same;—for instance, the letters *b s t*, when joined together will stand for *best* and *bust*, leaving the writer in deciphering to be guided by the context, which of those words, the characters were intended to express.

1	bsk	bask, busk,	49	hrdn	harden,
2	bst	best, bust,	50	hrvst	harvest,
3	bbl	babble, bubble,	51	jm	jam, jamb, gem,
4	blnk	blank, blink,	52	jt	jet, jot, jut,
5	brng	bring,	53	jgl	joggle, juggle,
6	be–km	became, become,	54	jmp	jump,
7	be–dk	bedeck,	55	jnk	junk,
8	be–hd	behead,	56	jrk	jerk,
9	be–nm	benumb,	57	jst	jest, just,
10	be–rft	bereft,	58	jrnl	journal,
11	be–st	besat, beset	59	jspr	jasper,
12	be–trst	betrust,	60	jngl	jangle, jingle, jungle
13	dmp	damp, dump,	61	kng	king,
14	drk	dark, dirk,	62	kmn	common,
15	drm	dram, drum,	63	krd	card, curd,
16	dsk	desk, disk, dusk,	64	krv	carve, curve,
17	dngr	danger,	65	kst	cast, cost,
18	dprt	depart, deport,	66	kptv	captive,
19	dsrt	desert, dessert,	67	kndl	candle, kindle,
20	dvrg	diverge,	68	knsl	cancel,
21	frm	farm, firm, form,	69	knsr	cancer,
22	fst	fast, fist, fust,	70	knvs	canvas, canvass,
23	frvd	fervid,	71	lft	left, lift, luft,
24	fstl	festal,	72	lmp	lamp, limp, lump,
25	frgt	forget, forgot,	73	lnd	land, lend,
26	fngr	finger,	74	lng	ling, long, lung,
27	frnd	friend,	75	lnk	lank, link,
28	frst	first, frost,	76	lnt	lent, lint, lunt,
29	frgv	forgave, forgive,	77	lftr	laughter, lifter,
30	fntm	phantom,	78	mnr	manner, manor,
31	gmp	gimp,	79	mrk	mark, marque,
32	gft	gift,	80	mmbr	member,
33	grd	gird, guard,	81	mngl	mangle, mingle,
34	gst	guest, gust,	82	mrtl	mortal, myrtle,
35	gvr	giver,	83	mrtr	martyr, mortar,
36	grft	graft,	84	mstr	master, muster,
37	grlnd	garland,	85	nn	none, nun,
38	grsp	grasp,	86	nmf	nymph,
39	gspl	gospel,	87	nml	animal, enamel,
40	gvrn	govern,	88	nrv	nerve,
41	hlp	help,	89	ngr	anger,
42	hnk	hank,	90	ntr	enter, inter,
43	hrm	harm,	91	nmbr	number,
44	hrp	harp,	92	pln	plan,
45	hsk	husk.	93	png	pang,
46	hndr	hinder,	94	pdlr	padler, pedlar,
47	hngr	hanger, hunger,	95	pndr	pander, ponder,
48	hrbr	harbor,	96	pnsl	pencil, pensile,

EXERCISE VI.   Continued.

97	prdn	pardon,	132	vsl	vassal, vessel,
98	qk	quack, quick,	133	vst	vast, vest,
99	qrl	quarrel, querl,	134	vxn	vixen,
100	qvr	quiver,	135	vlvt	velvet,
101	qntm	quantum,	136	vrmn	vermin,
102	qstn	question,	137	vrnl	vernal,
103	rnk	rank,	138	vstl	vestal,
104	rsk	risk, rusk,	139	wft	waft, weft,
105	rnsm	ransom,	140	wng	wing,
106	rstk	rustic,	141	wnt	want, went, wont,
107	re-dm	redeem,	142	wrk	work,
108	re fr	refer,	143	wrm	warm, worm,
109	re-grd	regard,	144	wlkm	welcome,
110	re-mrk	remark,	145	wndr	wander, wonder,
111	re-snt	recent, resent,	146	wsdm	wisdom,
112	re-trd	retard,	147	xs	excess,
113	snd	sand, send,	148	xmn	examine,
114	snt	cent, scent, sent,	149	xmt	exempt,
115	spl	spell, spill,	150	xpl	expel,
116	spr	spar, spur,	151	xst	exist,
117	swm	swam, swim, swum,	152	xpnd	expand, expend,
118	smpl	sample, simple,	153	xprs	express,
119	sstm	system,	154	xprt	expert, export,
120	stmp	stamp, stump,	155	xtnt	extant, extent,
121	stnd	stand, stunned,	156	yl	yell,
122	tkl	tackle, tickle,	157	ys	yes,
123	tng	tang, tongue, tung,	158	yt	yacht, yet,
124	trn	tern, torn, turn,	159	ylp	yelp,
125	tsk	task, tusk,	160	yng	young,
126	tmbr	tambor, timber,	161	yrd	yard,
127	tmpr	tamper, temper,	162	yrk	yerk,
128	tndr	tender, tinder,	163	yrn	yarn, yearn,
129	tngl	tangle, tingle,	164	zfr	zaffir, zephyr,
130	trmp	tramp tromp trump	165	znk	zinc,
131	vmp	vamp,	166	zst	zest,

EXERCISE VII.

1	chf	chaff, chuff,	21	thn	than, then, thin,
2	chp	chap, chip, chop,	22	thr	their, there,
3	cht	chat, chit,	23	ths	this, thus,
4	chmp	champ, chump,	24	thnk	thank, think,
5	chns	chance,	25	thrd	third, thread,
6	chnt	chant,	26	thndr	thunder,
7	chrm	charm,	27	thrft	thrift,
8	chrt	chart,	28	thrng	throng,
9	chst	chest,	29	thrsh	thrash thresh thrush
10	chptr	chapter,	30	thrst	thirst, thrust,
11	shn	shin, shun,	31	whf	whiff,
12	shd	shad, shed, shod,	32	whm	whim,
13	shp	ship, shop,	33	whn	when, whin,
14	shft	shaft, shift,	34	whr	where,
15	shlf	shelf,	35	wht	what, whet,
16	shrk	shark,	36	whlp	whelp,
17	shrp	sharp,	37	whns	whence,
18	shtr	shatter, shutter,	38	whrf	wharf,
19	shltr	shelter,	39	whrl	whirl,
20	shngl	shingle,	40	whspr	whisper,

KEY TO THE VOWEL CHARACTERS, &c.

		as heard in
ā	· · ·	age, ale, aim, bait, gate, lame, may, pray, save, whale, &c.
ă	· · ·	add, act, apt, ask, accept, assent, assume, assure, attend, &c.
ä	· · ·	alms, arch, ark, art, balm, calm, calf, cart, halve, psalm, &c.
à	· · ·	all, alter, ball, balk, call, false, hall, pall, small, tall, talk, &c.
ē	· · ·	eel, ear, eat, eve, beer, dear, flee, glee, he, knee, me, see, tea, &c.
ĕ	· · ·	ebb, edge, egg, ell, end, earl, earn, earth, elder, ever, &c.
ī	· · ·	idol, isle, ice, item, kite, lie, light, mite, night, sight, tile, &c.
ĭ	· · ·	ill, imp, inch, ink, it, itch, idiot, igneous, ignorant, iterate, &c.
ō	· · ·	own, opium, open, blow, flow, go, hole, lone, note, show, &c.
ŏ	· · ·	odd, offer, office, oft, often, olive, option, otter, oxen, oxygen, &c.
ō & ōō	· · ·	lose, move, prove, tomb, whom, food, gloom, moon, spoon, &c.
ū	· · ·	use, unit, unity, blue, due, flue, glue, hue, rue, sue, true, &c.
ŭ	· · ·	udder, ugly, ulcer, umber, uncle, under, upper, usher, &c.
oi & oy	· · ·	boy, boil, coy, coil, joy, join, oil, oint, oyster, toy, toil, &c.
ou & ow	· · ·	bough, doubt, down, fowl, now, owl, out, power, sour, tower, &c.

EXERCISE VIII.

VOWELS, DIPHTHONGS, DOUBLE CONSONANTS, &c.

Column labels: . × ! ? wh th sh sh ch ow&ou oi&oy ū ū ōō&ôô ō&ŏ ō ī ĭ ĕ ē ă&au ä ā ā

c 5

EXPOSITION OF THE VOWELS AND DIPHTHONGS.

A.

The long slender *ā* at the beginning of a word, as heard in *age, ale, aim, &c.*, is represented thus . Ex. *āp, ape;* *āt, ate, &c.*

The short Italian *ă*, at the beginning of a word, as heard in *add, act, ant, &c.*, is represented thus . Ex. *ănsr, answer;* *ătnd, attend, &c.*

The long slender, or short Italian *a*, occurring in the middle, or at the end of a word, may be expressed thus or thus . Ex. *dār, dare;* *fāth, faith;* *re-ăpr, reappear, &c.*

The long slender *ā* must be substituted for the diphthongs, *ai, au, ay, eu, ei,* and *ey*, in such words as *aid, gauge, nay, reign, prey, &c.*

The long Italian *ä*, at the beginning of a word, as heard in *alms, ardour, army, &c.*, is represented thus . Ex. *ärch,* *ärk, &c.*

The broad German *â, au,* and *aw*, at the

beginning of a word, must be expressed thus
P. Ex. ᶘ, *aul-tr*, for *altar* and *alter;*
ᶘ, *aul-thō, although, &c.*

The long Italian *ä*, the broad German *â*,
au, or *aw*, may be expressed thus ٩ or P,
when occurring in the middle, or at the end
of a word. Ex. ᷫ *bäm, balm;* ᷫ *käm,*
calm; ᷱ *dau-tr, daughter, &c.*

The long Italian *ä* must be substituted
for the diphthong *au*, in the words *aunt,*
daunt, flaunt, &c.

Oa and *ou*, have sometimes the sound of
au, and must be substituted by the latter
accordingly; writing *graut,* for *groat; saut,*
for *sought; thaut,* for *thought, &c.*

E.

The long sound of *ē*, at the beginning of
a word, as heard in *eagle, east, eat, &c.*, is
represented thus ᴧ. Ex. ᷲ *ēch, each;*
ᷔ *ēv, eve, &c.*

The short sound of *ĕ*, at the beginning of
a word, as heard in *ebb, edge, etch, &c.*, is
represented thus ᴄ. Ex. V *ĕr, err;* ᷴ
ĕrth, earth, &c.

The long or short *e*, occurring in the
middle or at the end of a word, may be ex-

pressed by either of the above characters. Ex. ∾ *dēr*, for *dear* and *deer* ; ∾ *fēr*, *fear* ; ⅄ *poët*, &c.

E must be substituted for the diphthongs, *ea, ee, ei, ey*, and *ie*, in the words, *beast, beer, ceil, key, liege*, &c.

I and *y* must be expressed by *ē*, in the words *fatigue, intrigue, marine, fancy, mercy*, &c.

The sound of *e*, forming a distinct sylla- ble, is represented by the same characters, having larger loops, thus ⌒, ⌒ ; writing *n-ē-mē*, for *enemy; m-ē-nence*, for *eminence*, &c.

I.

When the long diphthongal sound of *ī*, occurs at the beginning of a word, as heard in *ice, idol*, &c., it is represented thus ⌒. Ex. ⌒ *īrn, iron* ; ⌒ *ītm, item*, &c.

The short sound of *ĭ*, at the beginning of a word, as heard in *ill, imp, itch*, &c., is rep- resented thus ⌒. ⌒ *ĭnch*, ⌒ *ĭnk*, &c.

Either of the above characters may be used to represent the long or short sound of *i*, when occurring in the middle, or at the end of a word. Ex. ⌒ *līt, light*, ⌒ *nī, nigh*, &c.

The diphthongs *ei, eye, ie, ui,* and *uy,* also *y,* must be substituted by the letter *i,* in such words as *height, eyelid, lie, guide, buy, type, tyrant,* &c.

O.

The long open *ō,* at the beginning of a word, as heard in *ode, old, ore,* &c., is represented thus ⟨. Ex. ⟨ *ōn, own ;* ⟨ *ōpn, open,* &c.

The short *ŏ* at the beginning of a word, as heard in *object, observe, obtain,* &c., is represented thus ⟨. Ex. ⟨ *ŏfr, offer ;* ⟨ *ŏp-tk, optic,* &c.

The long or short sound of *o,* when occurring in the middle, or at the end of a word, may be represented by either of the above characters, as in the following examples ; ⟨ *nōt,* ⟨ *sōl,* &c.

The long open *ō,* must be substituted for *oa, oe, oo, ou, ow, ew,* and *eau;* in the words *boar, doe, floor, pour, slow, shew, beau,* &c.

The long close *ó* and *óó,* as heard in *lose, prove, cool, room, spoon,* &c., may be expressed thus ⟨ or ⟨. Ex. ⟨ *móóv, move ;* ⟨ *móón, moon ;* ⟨ *sóón, soon,* &c.

The long close *ó* may be substituted for the diphthongs, *eu, oe,* and *ou,* in the words *rheum, shoe, tour,* &c.

U.

The long sound of *ū,* at the beginning of a word, as heard in *unity, utility,* &c, is represented thus Ʂ. Ex. Ʂ *ūs, use;* Ꞔ *ūnit, unite,* &c.

The short sound of *ŭ,* at the beginning of a word, as heard in *umber, uncle, urgent,* &c., is represented thus ℓ. Ex. Ʂ *ŭlsr, ulcer;* ℓ *ŭtr, utter,* &c.

The long or short sound of *u,* occurring in the middle, or at the end of a word, may be expressed by either of the above characters, as in the following examples; Ꞔ *mūt, mute;* ℓ *nū, new,* &c.

U may be substituted for *eu, ew, ue, ieu,* and *iew,* in such words as *feud, few, glue, lieu, view,* &c.

U must be omitted in the words *fatigue, intrigue, oblique,* &c.

Oi and Oy.

The sound of the diphthongs *oi* and *oy,* as heard in *boy, boil, coy, coil,* &c., is represented thus *9* or *ρ*; whichever combines most easily with the preceding character. Ex. *joy*, *loin*, &c.

Ou and Ow.

The diphthongs *ou* and *ow*, as heard in *hour, sour, bower, tower, &c.*, are expressed thus *⊃* or *C*; as may be found most easy to combine with the preceding or following character. Ex. *mouth*, *now*, &c.

EXERCISE IX.

1	ăd	aid,	34	aul	all, awl,	
2	āk	ache, ake,	35	aun	awn,	
3	āl	ail, ale,	36	aubrn	auburn,	
4	ām	aim,	37	augst	august,	
5	bāl	bail, bale,	38	aultr	altar, alter,	
6	dā	day,	39	aulthō	although,	
7	fān	fain, fane, feign,	40	authr	author,	
8	fār	fair, fare,	41	autm	autumn,	
9	hāl	hail, hale,	42	baul	ball, bawl,	
10	māl	mail, male,	43	baut	bought,	
11	nā	nay, neigh,	44	dautr	daughter,	
12	pār	pair, pare, pear,	45	haul	hall, haul,	
13	rān	rain, rein, reign,	46	kaut	caught,	
14	slā	slate, slay, sleigh,	47	lau	law,	
15	vān	vain, vane, vein,	48	naut	naught, nought,	
16	wā	way, weigh,	49	saut	sought,	
17	ăd	add,	50	taut	taught,	
18	ădū	adieu,	51	thaut	thought,	
19	ăfx	affix,	52	tauk	talk,	
20	ăpt	apt,	53	wauk	walk,	
21	ăd–mt	admit,	54	ēl	eel,	
22	ăsnt	ascent, assent,	55	ĕr	ear,	
23	ătmt	attempt,	56	ĕt	eat,	
24	ătnd	attend,	57	ēgr	eager,	
25	ärbr	arbor,	58	bēr	beer, bier,	
26	ärmĕ	army,	59	bēt	beat, beet,	
27	ärktk	arctic,	60	dēr	dear, deer,	
28	bä	baa,	61	flā	flea, flee,	
29	bäm	balm,	62	hēl	heal, heel,	
30	häf	half,	63	hēr	hear, here,	
31	käm	calm,	64	mēt	meat, meet, mete,	
32	päm	palm,	65	nēd	knead, need,	
33	säv	salve,	66	rēd	read, reed,	

EXERCISE IX. Continued.

67	sē	sea, see,	127	lōōs	loose, lose,
68	sēn	scene, seen, seine,	128	mōōn	moon,
69	tēm	team, teem,	129	mōōv	move,
70	ĕb	ebb,	130	pōōr	poor,
71	ĕg	egg,	131	rōōm	room, rheum,
72	ĕl	ell,	132	shōō	shoe,
73	ĕlm	elm,	133	skōōl	school,
74	ĕrn	earn,	134	sōōp	soup,
75	ĕrl	earl,	135	tōō	too, two,
76	ĕsā	essay,	136	tōōr	tour,
77	īdl	idle, idol,	137	ūnt	unit,
78	irn	iron,	138	ūs	use,
79	ītm	item,	139	ūsrp	usurp,
80	bīt	bight, bite,	140	blū	blew, blue,
81	hī	hie, high,	141	dū	dew, due,
82	hīt	height, hight,	142	flu	flew, flue,
83	līr	liar, lier, lyre,	143	krūl	crewel, cruel,
84	mīt	might, mite,	144	lū	lieu,
85	nīt	knight, night,	145	mūs	muse,
86	sīn	sign, sine,	146	pūpl	pupil,
87	slīt	sleight, slight,	147	tūtr	tutor,
88	tīm	thyme, time,	148	ŭdr	udder,
89	thī	thigh, thy,	149	ŭlsr	ulcer,
90	ll	ill,	150	ŭpr	upper,
91	ĭmp	imp,	151	ŭrchn	urchin,
92	ĭnk	ink,	152	ŭshr	usher,
93	ĭstms	isthmus,	153	ŭtmst	utmost,
94	ĭtch	itch,	154	boi	boy,
95	ōn	own,	155	boil	boil,
96	ōpm	opium,	156	foil	foil,
97	ōpn	open,	157	hoist	hoist,
98	ōr	oar, o'er, ore,	158	joi	joy,
99	bō	beau, bōw,	159	joint	joint,
100	bōr	boar, bore,	160	loin	loin,
101	dō	doe, dough,	161	nois	noise,
102	fōr	fore, four,	162	oil	oil,
103	lō	lo, low,	163	oint	oint,
104	pōr	pore, pour,	164	oistr	oyster,
105	rōd	road, rode,	165	point	point,
106	rōt	rote, wrote,	166	soil	soil,
107	slō	sloe, slow,	167	toi	toy,
108	sō	so, sow, sew,	168	toil	toll,
109	sōl	sole, soul,	169	void	void,
110	tō	to, toe, tōw,	170	vois	voice,
111	ōbtn	obtain,	171	bou	bough, bōw,
112	ōptk	optic,	172	bour	bower,
113	ōprs	oppress,	173	dout	doubt,
114	ōprä	opera,	174	foul	foul, fowl,
115	ōfr	offer,	175	hous	house,
116	ōfsr	officer,	176	loud	loud,
117	ōrbt	orbit,	177	mouth	mouth,
118	ōrdl	ordeal,	178	nou	now,
119	ōrdr	order,	179	oul	owl,
120	ōrdn	ordain,	180	out	out,
121	ōrfn	orphan,	181	pour	power,
122	ōrgn	organ,	182	sour	sour,
123	fōōd	food,	183	tour	tower,
124	glōōm	gloom,	184	trout	trout,
125	hōōp	hoop,	185	vou	vow,
126	kōōk	cook,	186	vouch	vouch, &c.

DIRECTIONS FOR STUDYING THE THREE FOLLOWING EXERCISES.

The Learner having attentively perused the contents of the preceding pages, must next commit to memory the various words which each Stenographic letter denotes when standing alone. It will be necessary to acquire the most perfect familiarity with these characters, and the words which they respectively represent, so as to be able to apply them immediately, without having occasion to refer to the Guide.

It will be observed on examining the following tables, that each character denotes two or more of the most common words of which it forms the initial, or in which it is a prominent letter; as for example, the character ⌒ *m*, stands for *am*, *me*, *my*, and *may*; leaving the context to point out in deciphering, which of those words it was intended to express.

EXAMPLES.

I will do that for you. Would you not

do it for me ? You may do it again if you

will. If he be in, I will go up. Who is it ?

It is he .   Let us go in .   Will you go

with me ? May he not go with us ? Has

he ever been with you ? I believe not.

You may do as you like.   I shall go. I

know that you can go. He is gone. They

will go . Have they not been ? They were

to have gone. I believe they will employ

you for that. Do you not believe so ?

EXERCISE X.

The consonants, and the words they denote when standing alone.

B	⟨	Be, been.
D	╱	Do, does, done.
F¹	᠊	For, of
F²	᠊	From, if.
G	᠊	Go, goes, gone.
H¹	⌒	Has, hast, have.
H²	⌣	He, had, hadst.
J	᠊	Just, judge.
K¹	᠊	Can, canst.
K²	᠊	Could, couldst.
L	⟩	All, love, loves.
M	⌢	Am, me, my, may.
N	⌣	In, on, not, no.
P	╲	Praise, pray, prayer.
Q	᠊	Quite, quiet, quantity.
R	⟨	Are, art, or.
S	│	So, is, as, us.
T	—	To, it, at, the.
V¹	᠊	Very, verily.
V²	᠊	Virtue, virtuous.
W¹	᠊	Was, with, will.
W²	᠊	We, were, would.
X¹	᠊	Exceed, except.
X²	᠊	Expect, example.
Y	⟩	Ye, you, your, yours.
Z	⟨	Zeal, zealot, zealous.

EXERCISE XI.

The vowels and diphthongs, and the words they denote
when standing alone.

A 1	૧	A, any.
A 2	ρ	Again, against.
A 3	૧	Ah, ay, aye.
A 4	ρ	Awe, also.
E 1	ᴕ	Evil, evils.
E 2	ᴦ	Ever, every.
E 3	ᴕ	Even, evening—s.
E 4	ᴦ	Err, error, errors.
I 1	૭	I, eye.
I 2	ρ	Its, itself.
Oi 1	૭	Destroy, destroys.
Oi 2	ρ	Employ, employs.
O 1	૮	O, oh, owe.
O 2	૮	Off, oft, often.
Oo 1	૮	Other, others.
Oo 2	૮	Otherguise, otherwise.
U 1	૭	Usual, usually.
U 2	℮	Up, upon.
Ou 1	૭	Hour, hours, hourly.
Ou 2	℃	Our, ours, ourselves.

EXERCISE XII.

The double consonants, and the words they denote when standing alone.

Ch	✓	Much, such.
Sh ¹		Shall, shalt.
Sh ²		Should, shouldst.
Th	—	Thee, they, that.
Wh	·ſ	Who, why, which.

Characters not included in the preceding Tables, and the words they denote when standing alone.

1	.	An, and.
2	○	One, once.
3		After, afterwards.
4		Fore, forwards.
5		Over, o'er.
6		Under.
7		Above.
8		Below, beneath.
9		Belief, believe—s.
10		Large, let, like.
11		Know, knows.
12		Knew, known.
13		Alway, always.
14		Might, might'st.

PUNCTUATION, ETC.

A comma, semicolon, and colon, are represented in Short-Hand (as in common writing,) by their usual marks. A period or
full stop is denoted by a small cross thus ×
(repeating the cross twice at the end of a
paragraph.) A note of interrogation thus ·| .
A note of admiration thus |·. Viz. or name-
ly, is denoted by a mark thus ⊣. Etc. or &c.
by a mark the reverse of the latter, thus ⊢ .

ON PROPER NAMES.

The names of persons, places, &c., must
have a mark thus ` , placed immediately
over them as ℰ Byron, ℧ Milton, ℈ Pope,
℥ London, ℞ York, &c.

All words alluding to the Deity, may in
general be expressed by their initial and a
mark thus ′ placed over them as ⸴ Lord,
⌣ God, &c.

EXERCISE XIII.

The Lord is good *to all* . Trust *in the Lord*

and do good . *In thee, O Lord, do I* put *my*

trust. *If God be for us, who can be against*

us ? *I will* sing *praise to* thy name *O thou*

Most High . *By the* fear *of the Lord* men

depart *from evil.* Turn thou *me and I*

shall be turned, *for* thou *art the Lord my*

God . *I will praise the* name *of the Lord.*

Pray one for another . Help *us, O Lord,*

our God, *for we* rest on thee . *So shall*

we ever be with the Lord . Pray for us .

EXERCISE XIV.

As thy days, so shall thy strength be.
As thī dās, *so shall* thī strngth *be.*

Hold thou me up, and I shall be safe. Lord
Hōld thou *me up, and I shall be* sāf. *Lord*

increase our faith. All things are yours.
n-krēs *our* fāth. *All* thngs *are yours.*

My sheep hear my voice and I know them
My shēp hēr *my* vois *and I know* them

and they follow me. What time I am afraid,
and they fl-lō *me.* Wht tīm *I am* ăfrād,

I will trust in thee. He will keep the feet
I will trst *in thee. He will* kēp *the* fēt

of his saints. If thou seek him, he will be
of hs sānts. *If* thou sēk hm, *he will be*

found of thee ; but if thou forsake him, he
found *of thee;* bt *if* thou fr-sk hm, *he*

will cast thee off for ever. Though he slay
will kst *thee off for ever.* Thō *he* slā

me, yet will I trust in him. He shall deliver
me, yt *will I* trst *in* hm. *He shall* dlvr

thee from all evil. Rejoice evermore. Thou
thee from all evil. Re-jois *ever* mōr. Thou

Lord, hast not forsaken them that seek thee.
Lord, hast not frskn thm *that* sēk *thee.*

Show me thy ways, O Lord, teach me thy
Shō *me* thī wās , *O Lord,* tēch *me* thī

paths.   Except a man be born again, he can-
pths .   *Except a* mn *be* brn *again, he can*

not see the kingdom of God.   How sweet
not sē *the*   kngdm *of God.*   Hou   swt

are thy words unto my taste ! yea, sweeter
are thī wrds   ntō *my* tāst *!* yā ,   swtr

than honey to my mouth.   Blessed are the
thn . hōnē *to my* mouth.   Blsd   *are the*

pure in heart, for they shall see God.   Wo
pūr *in* hrt . *for they shall* sē *God.*   Wō

unto the wicked ; it shall be ill with him.
ntō   *the   wkd   ; it shall be* ĭl *with* hm.

We which have believed, do enter into rest.
We which have be-lvd , *do* ntr ntō rst .

If we say that we have not sinned, we make
If we sā *that we have not* snd , *we* mk

him a liar, and his word is not in us.   We
hm *a* līr , *and* hs . wrd *is not in us.*   *We*

love him, because he first loved us.   Hold
lov hm , be-kaus *he* frst lovd *us.*   Hōld

that fast which thou hast, that no man take
that fst *which* thou *hast, that no* mn tk

thy crown.   The Lord is my defence, and
thī kroun.   *The Lord is my*   dfns , *and*

D

my God is the rock of my refuge.   In God
my God is the rk *of my* rfūg .   *In God*

have I put my trust, I will not be afraid
have I pt *my* trst , *I will not be* ăfrād

what man can do unto me.   Fight the good
wht   mn *can do* ntō *me.*   Fīt *the* gd

fight of faith, lay hold on eternal life.   Resist
fīt *of* fāth, lā hōld *on* ētrnl līf.   Re-sst

the devil, and he will flee from you.   Heal
the dvl , *and he will* flē *from you.*   .Hēl

me, O Lord, and I shall be healed ; save me
me, O Lord, and I shall be hēld ; sāv *me*

.and I shall be saved ; for thou art my praise.
and I shall be sāvd ; *for* thou *art my* prās .

EXERCISE XV.

Then shall we know if we follow on to know
Thn *shall we know, if we* fl-lō *on to know*

the Lord.   The meek shall increase their joy
the Lord. The mēk *shall* n-krēs thr   joi

in the Lord.   The Lord of hosts is with us,
in the Lord.   The Lord of hōsts *is with us,*

the God of Jacob is our refuge.   I wait for
the God of Jākb *is our*   rfūg .   *I* wāt *for*

the Lord, my soul doth wait and in his word
the Lord, my sōl dth   wāt *and in* hs   wrd

do I hope. Rejoice not against me, O mine
do I hōp . Re-jois *not against me, O* mīn

enemy; when I fall I shall arise.
n-ē-mē; whn *I* faul *I shall* ărīs .

My yoke is easy and my burden is light.
My yōk *is* ē-sē *and my* brdn *is* līt .

Fear not, for I have redeemed thee; I have
Fēr *not, for I have* re-dmd *thee; I have*

called thee by thy name, thou art mine. So
kauld *thee* bī thī nm , thou *art* mīn . *So*

run that ye may obtain. The needy shall
rn *that ye may* ŏbtn . *The* nē-dē *shall*

not alway be forgotten. The Lord is my
not alway be frgtn . *The Lord is my*

rock, and my fortress, and my deliverer.
rk , *and my* frtrs , *and my* dlvrr .

Teach me thy way, O Lord, and lead me in
Tēch *me* thī wā, *O Lord, and* lēd *me in*

a plain path. Hide not thy face far from me,
ā plān pth . Hīd *not* thī fās fr *from me,*

put not thy servant away in anger. This
pt *not* thī srvnt āwā *in* ngr . Ths

God is our God, he will be our guide, even
God is our God, he will be our gīd , *even*

unto death. The just shall live by faith
ntō dth . *The just shall* lv *by* fāth.

REPETITION OF WORDS OR SENTENCES.

A dash thus —— drawn under a word or sentence, denotes an immediate repetition of the same.   Ex. ⟩ *Lord, Lord.*   ᴖ ⟩ *Turn ye, turn ye.*   ╲ ⟩ − ⟩ × *Praise ye the Lord. Praise ye the Lord,* &c.

When the particles *and, of, in, &c* , intervene, the repetition is denoted by placing a mark thus ⌐⎯⎯⎯⌐ under the word so repeated. Ex. ᴈ *Ever and ever.*   − ⟩ *The Lord of lords.* ᴄ ⟅ *From day to day,* &c.

If part of a sentence is to be repeated after something else has occurred, make a mark thus ⌐⎯⎯⎯ under the words to be repeated, and place a caret (ʌ) where the repetition is required. Thus ⎮ − ᴄ − ᴠⴭ ╲ ⟨ ⅔ , ⅔ ʌ ·⎮ *Is it just the innocent should be* condemned, *is it just the innocent should be reviled ?*

It may be here remarked, that in the practice of Short-Hand it will frequently be necessary to make use of the caret, (ʌ) to imply any defect in the writing; as words are sometimes entirely lost, from the sudden lowering of the speaker's voice, or other cause of interruption.

EXERCISE XVI.

1	Lord, Lord.	29	Line upon line.
2	Moses, Moses.	30	Eye for eye.
3	Saul, Saul.	31	Tooth for tooth.
4	Hark ! hark !	32	The Lord of lords.
5	Verily, verily.	33	The God of gods.
6	Welcome, welcome.	34	The King of kings.
7	My Father, My Father.	35	For ever and ever.
8	Turn ye, turn ye. [Lord.	36	From hour to hour.
9	Praise ye the Lord, praise ye the	37	From day to day.
10	Glory, glory, glory.	38	From week to week.
11	Holy, holy, holy.	39	From month to month.
12	Amen and Amen.	40	From year to year.
13	Again and again.	41	From time to time.
14	Ever and ever.	42	From town to town.
15	By-and-by.	43	From place to place.
16	Better and better.	44	From sport to sport.
17	Worse and worse.	45	From guest to guest.
18	More and more.	46	From face to face.
19	Less and less.	47	From hand to hand.
20	Higher and higher.	48	From mouth to mouth.
21	Lower and lower.		
22	Richer and richer.		
23	Poorer and poorer.		
24	Harder and harder.		
25	Softer and softer.		
26	Round and round.		
27	All in all.		
28	Hand in hand.		

Whatsoever things are true, *whatsoever things are* honest, *whatsoever things are* just, *whatsoever things are* pure, *whatsoever things are* lovely, *whatsoever things are* of good report. *If there be any* virtue, *if there be any* praise, think on these things.

WORDS OF CONTRARY SIGNIFICATION.

An oblique line thus / when placed after a word, denotes an opposition of meaning, as in the following examples. ⁊/ *good and bad;* ⌣ℓ/ *high and low, &c.*

An oblique line, with a curve to the right, thus / is used to express a word of opposite meaning, joined with the former by the conjunction *or.* Ex. ⁊/ *good or bad;* ⌐ƒ *truth or falsehood, &c.*

The negative particles, *dis, il, im, in, ir, un, &c.,* may be represented by an oblique line placed before the remainder of the word. Ex. /ᴖ *dis-own;* /⌐ʌ *dis-trust;* /ᴄ *un-even;* /ℓ *un-known;* /ᴐ *un-usual;* /ʔ *un-quiet;* /ᴸ *un-expressed, &c.*

EXERCISE XVII.

1	Heaven and earth	25	The just and the unjust
2	Earth and heaven	26	The learned and the unlearned
3	Day and night	27	From east to west
4	Light and dark	28	From north to south
5	Life and death	29	From one to another
6	Old and young	30	Good or bad
7	Young and old	31	Light or dark
8	Rich and poor	32	Fine or coarse
9	High and low	33	Strength or weakness
10	Long and short	34	Truth and falsehood
11	Thick and thin	35	This or that
12	Far and near	36	These or those
13	To and fro	37	Better or worse
14	Top and bottom	38	Well or ill
15	Up and down	39	High or low
16	Here and there	40	Rich or poor
17	Summer and winter	41	Boy or girl
18	Certain and uncertain	42	Land or water
19	Known and unknown	43	Over or under
20	Father and mother	44	Above or below
21	Brother and sister	45	Behind or before
22	Lady and gentleman	46	Inside or outside
23	Men and women	47	Within or without
24	A man and a woman	48	Long or short

EXERCISE XVIII.

1	*Dis*-agree	22	*In*-active	43	*Un*-chain
2	*Dis*-allow	23	*In*-animate	44	*Un*-changed
3	*Dis*-annul	24	*In*-attentive	45	*Un*-civil
4	*Dis*-array	25	*In*-definite	46	*Un*-clasp
5	*Dis*-believe	26	*In*-delicate	47	*Un*-easy
6	*Dis*-embark	27	*In*-disposed	48	*Un*-explained
7	*Dis*-honest	28	*In*-human	49	*Un*-fair
8	*Dis*-honour	29	*Ir*-regular	50	*Un*-fit
9	*Dis*-mount	30	*Ir*-religion	51	*Un*-fixed
10	*Dis*-member	31	*Ir*-resolute	52	*Un*-foreseen
11	*Il*-legal	32	*Ir*-reverent	53	*Un*-fortunate
12	*Il*-liberal	33	*Ir*-relevant	54	*Un*-furnished
13	*Il*-licit	34	*Un*-altered	55	*Un*-just
14	*Il*-literate	35	*Un*-bent	56	*Un*-kind
15	*Im*-mature	36	*Un*-biassed	57	*Un*-known
16	*Im*-moderate	37	*Un*-blest	58	*Un*-learned
17	*Im*-modest	38	*Un*-born	59	*Un*-limited
18	*Im*-moral	39	*Un*-buckle	60	*Un*-married
19	*Im*-mortal	40	*Un*-burden	61	*Un*-safe
20	*Im*-polite	41	*Un*-caught	02	*Un*-seen
21	*Im*-pure	42	*Un*-certain	63	*Un*-worthy

PREFIXES AND TERMINATIONS.*

The Learner having been led by progres-
sive exercises, from the simple characters,
to the writing of plain Scripture sentences,
it will be necessary to turn the attention to
the Stenographic characters used to represent prefixes and terminations, a matter of
great importance in the brevity and legibility
of Short-Hand. The readiest mode of
designating these is, in some cases, to use
simple arbitrary signs, and in others, the
letters of the Stenographic Alphabet, with
certain points to be explained hereafter.

A small circle thus ₒ when placed immediately over any word, denotes the prefix
over, as in ᴄ *over-come ;* ᴜ *over-take, &c.*

The same character when placed under a
word, denotes the prefix *under,* as in ᴄ
under-go ; ᴜ *under-take, &c.*

The terminations *ing, cian, cion, sion,
tion, ceous, cious,* and *tious,* are to be ex-

* The prefixes and terminations here made use of,
have been chosen entirely with a view to suit the convenience of Stenography, without any reference to the
derivation of words.

pressed in the following manner. *Ing*, forming a distinct syllable at the *end* of a word, is represented by adding a small circle to the right* of the last point in the preceding character, as in the following examples : ℰ *ĕr-ing, erring* ; ℰ *kr-ing, caring*, &c.

Cian, cion, sion, and *tion*, pronounced like *shun* and *ceous, cious* and *tious*, pronounced like *shus*, may be represented by a small circle turned on the left side* of the last point of the preceding character, as in the following examples. ℰ *pr-shun, portion* ; ℰ *vr-shun, version* ; ℰ *x-m-shun, exemption* ; ℰ *grā-shus, gracious* ; ℰ *spā-shus, spacious*, &c. *Sician* and *sition*, pronounced like *zishun*, may be represented by a circle, twice the size of that used for *shun*, attached to the last point of the preceding character, as before. Examples. ℰ *mū-zishun, musician* ; ℰ *po-zishun, position*, &c.

Ous, when forming a separate syllable, must be expressed by a small stroke, made

---

* In horizontal characters, the top is to be considered the left hand side, and the bottom the right. Ex. ℰ *p-t-tion, petition* ; ℰ *gt-ing, getting*, &c.

through the preceding letter, as in the following examples : *co-p-ous*, *copious* ;
tm-r-ous, *timorous*, &c.

When a character of the Alphabet is
intended to represent a *prefix*, it must be
distinguished by having a *comma* placed
under it, as in the following examples :
discon-tnt, for *discontent* ; *trans-fr*, for
transfer, &c.

A character used to express a *termination*,
must be distinguished by having a *period*
placed *under* it, as in the following examples : *gm-ble*, for *gamble* ; *d-mand*,
for *demand* ; *pā-ment*, for *payment*, &c.

When the first character of a word is intended to represent a *prefix*, and the last a
termination, a single point must be placed
over the word, instead of inserting a comma and a period beneath ; as in the following examples : *con-duct* ; *inter-po-
sition*, *interposition* ; *temp-r-ance*, *tem-
perance*, &c.

When the learner has occasion to express
in Short-Hand, a word containing two of
such terminations as have been selected, the
first must be spelt according to its sound,

and the last denoted by its usual mark, placing the period as in the preceding rule. Examples ~⤬ *com-mnd-ment, commandment;* ⤳ *con-frm-ing, con-firm-ing,* &c.

When the termination of any word may be expressed by either of the before-mentioned characters, the plural is formed by converting the point into a short perpendicular stroke, thus: ⤳ *com-ms-sions, commissions;* ⤳ *pe-t-tions, petitions;* ⤳ *sn-t-ments, sentiments,* &c.

EXERCISE XIX.

1	over–awe	21	over–rule	41	under–hand
2	over–bear	22	over–run	42	under–keeper
3	over–bid	23	over–see	43	under–laid
4	over–blow	24	over–sight	44	under–lay
5	over–board	25	over–sleep	45	under–let
6	over–burden	26	over–stock	46	under–rate
7	over–cast	27	over–strew	47	under–mine
8	over–charge	28	over–sway	48	under–neath
9	over–come	29	over–take	49	under–rate
10	over–draw	30	over–taken	50	under–sell
11	over–flow	31	over–throw	51	under–stand
12	over–grow	32	over–turn	52	under–stood
13	over–hang	33	over–weight	53	under–take
14	over–hear	34	over–whelm	54	under–taker
15	over–lay	35	under–bid	55	under–taken
16	over–load	36	under–bred	56	under–value
17	over–look	37	under–drain	57	under–went
18	over–pay	38	under–foot	58	under–work
19	over–power	39	under–go	59	under–write
20	over–reach	40	under–grown	60	under–written

EXERCISE XX.

1	beam-*ing*	51	deten-*tion*	101	avari-*cious*
2	bear-*ing*	52	divi-*sion*	102	effica-*tious*
3	bit-*ing*	53	diver-*sion*	103	cultiva-*tion*
4	cant-*ing*	54	devo-*tion*	104	delibera-*tion*
5	card-*ing*	55	dona-*tion*	105	desola-*tion*
6	dar-*ing*	56	edi-*tion*	106	desolu-*tion*
7	do-*ing*	57	emo-*tion*	107	examina-*tion*
8	doubt-*ing*	58	exemp-*tion*	108	execu-*tion*
9	dur-*ing*	59	expres-*sion*	109	exporta-*tion*
10	fear-*ing*	60	founda-*tion*	110	habita-*tion*
11	fly-*ing*	61	impres-*sion*	111	importa-*tion*
12	giv-*ing*	62	inser-*tion*	112	invita-*tion*
13	go-*ing*	63	inten-*tion*	113	medita-*tion*
14	grow-*ing*	64	lega-*tion*	114	modera-*tion*
15	hear-*ing*	65	narra-*tion*	115	restora-*tion*
16	herr-*ing*	66	opti-*cian*	116	saluta-*tion*
17	hop-*ing*	67	parti-*tion*	117	valua-*tion*
18	learn-*ing*	68	peti-*tion*	118	visita-*tion*
19	liv-*ing*	69	planta-*tion*	119	phy-*sician*
20	mend-*ing*	70	pollu-*tion*	120	mu-*sician*
21	mourn-*ing*	71	posses-*sion*	121	po-*sition*
22	part-*ing*	72	quota-*tion*	122	impo-*sition*
23	pass-*ing*	73	redemp-*tion*	123	expo-*sition*
24	oppos-*ing*	74	rela-*tion*	124	oppo-*sition*
25	possess-*ing*	75	remis-*sion*	125	requi-*sition*
26	rend-*ing*	76	reten-*tion*	126	amor-*ous*
27	ring-*ing*	77	revi-*sion*	127	beaute-*ous*
28	send-*ing*	78	salva-*tion*	128	bounte-*ous*
29	sing-*ing*	79	sensa-*tion*	129	copi-*ous*
30	talk-*ing*	80	solu-*tion*	130	curi-*ous*
31	tak-*ing*	81	stagna-*tion*	131	danger-*ous*
32	turn-*ing*	82	taxa-*tion*	132	devi-*ous*
33	wadd-*ing*	83	voca-*tion*	133	dubi-*ous*
34	wad-*ing*	84	gra-*cious*	134	dute-*ous*
35	want-*ing*	85	spa-*cious*	135	fam-*ous*
36	warn-*ing*	86	pre-*cious*	136	furi-*ous*
37	wash-*ing*	87	atro-*cious*	137	gener-*ous*
38	lo-*tion*	88	auda-*cious*	138	lumin-*ous*
39	mo-*tion*	89	auspi-*cious*	139	mutin-*ous*
40	no-*tion*	90	capa-*cious*	140	numer-*ous*
41	po-*tion*	91	capri-*cious*	141	odi-*ous*
42	por-*tion*	92	deli-*cious*	142	pi-*ous*
43	pen-*sion*	93	falla-*cious*	143	raven-*ous*
44	pas-*sion*	94	fero-*cious*	144	seri-*ous*
45	na-*tion*	95	judi-*cious*	145	spuri-*ous*
46	op-*tion*	96	licen-*tious*	146	studi-*ous*
47	sec-*tion*	97	offi-*cious*	147	tedi-*ous*
48	ver-*sion*	98	rapa-*cious*	148	timor-*ous*
49	ascen-*sion*	99	saga-*cious*	149	vari-*ous*
50	dimen-*sion*	100	tena-*cious*	150	venom-*ous*

EXERCISE XXI.

ꟼ	ab, abbre, abro, abso,
ꝑ	advan, adven, adver, advo,
╱	discom, discon, disen, disin,
⌒	equi, equiv,
☌	affec, affirm,
☍	afflic, effec,
↩	aggra, aggre, agree, agri,
⌒	hyper, hyster,
◡	hydro, hypo,
ꝯ	imper, incom, incon, incor,
⌒	com, compre, compri, compro,
℧	con, contra, contri, contro,
⌒	magni, miscon, misin, multi,
◡	enter, inter, intro, intru,
⟋	ob, obsti, omni, oppor, oppro,
╲	per, pre, pri, pro, pur,
╱	recom, recon, repre, repro,
│	sub, subter, sup, super,
—	temp, tempt, tran, trans,
⌐	exer, extir, extra, expli.

EXERCISE XXII.

TERMINATIONS,
Represented by Alphabetical Characters.

૧ ρ	act, acted, actly, ance, ant, antly.
⊂	ble, bled, bly, bility, bilities.
/	dance, dant, dence, dent, dict, duct.
⊼ ⋋	ence, ency, ent, ently, est, eth, ever.
ᠳ ᠺ	fect, flect, flict, form, ful, fully.
⌣	grance, grant, graph, graphic,—al, guish.
⌒ ⌣	hend, hended, hensive, hibit, hood.
૭ ρ	ify, ifies, ity, ities, ety, eties.
⌐	ject, jest, join, journ, judge, just.
๓ ᧒	claim, cline, clude, clusive, count.
)	ly, liness, less, lessly, lect, lected.
⌒	mand, mend, mence, ment, mental.
⌣	nance, nant, nence, nent, nect, ness.
＼	place, plant, plete, point, prove.
૧	quence, quent, quently, quest, quish, quit.
⟨	racy, ract, rect, rance, rant, rupt.
|	scribe, script, spect, struct, suade.
—	tude, tute, tinct, tract, trict.
ᠳ ᠺ	vent, verse, vert, vest, vict, volve.
๓ ᧒ ⌣	ward, wards, warded, warder, wardeth.
⌒	sier, zier, sure, surely, zure.
⌣	chew, tue, tues, ture, teous, tuous,-ly.
╱ ＼	cial, sial, tial, science, tience, cient, tient.

EXERCISE XXIII.

1	*abbre*-viate	61	*con*-ceit	121	*per*-vade
2	*abro*-gate	62	*con*-cern	122	*pre*-face
3	*abso*-lute	63	*con*-cord	123	*pre*-fer
4	*advan*-tage	64	*con*-cur	124	*pre*-fix
5	*adver*-tise	65	*con*-demn	125	*pre*-serve
6	*advo*-cate	66	*con*-dense	126	*pre*-tend
7	*discom*-mode	67	*con*-dole	127	*pre*-tence
8	*discom*-pose	68	*con*-fer	128	*pre*-text
9	*discon*-cert	69	*con*-fess	129	*pre*-vail
10	*discon*-solate	70	*con*-fine	130	*pre*-vent
11	*discon*-tent	71	*con*-firm	131	*pri*-vate
12	*discon*-tinue	72	*con*-fuse	132	*pro*-cure
13	*disen*-gage	73	*con*-fute	133	*pro*-duce
14	*disen*-tangle	74	*con*-geal	134	*pro*-fane
15	*disin*-ter	75	*con*-sent	135	*pro*-fess
16	*disin*-thrall	76	*con*-serve	136	*pro*-gress
17	*equi*-distant	77	*con*-sign	137	*pro*-long
18	*equi*-poise	78	*con*-sist	138	*pro*-mote
19	*equi*-page	79	*con*-sole	139	*pro*-voke
20	*equiv*-ocal	80	*con*-sult	140	*pur*-sue
21	*equiv*-ocate	81	*con*-tain	141	*pur*-suit
22	*affec*-ted	82	*con*-temn	142	*pur*-vey
23	*affirm*-ative	83	*con*-tempt	143	*recom*-bine
24	*afflic*-ted	84	*con*-tent	144	*recom*-mit
25	*affec*-tive	85	*con*-test	145	*recom*-pact
26	*aggra*-vate	86	*con*-tinue	146	*recom*-pense
27	*aggre*-gate	87	*magni*-fy	147	*recom*-pose
28	*agri*-culture	88	*magni*-fier	148	*recon*-cile
29	*agri*-mony	89	*miscon*-ceive	149	*recon*-sider
30	*hyper*-bole	90	*miscon*-strue	150	*recon*-vene
31	*hyper*-critic	91	*misin*-fer	151	*recon*-vey
32	*hyster*-ical	92	*multi*-ply	152	*repre*-sent
33	*hydro*-gen	93	*multi*-plier	153	*repro*-bate
34	*hydro*-mel	94	*enter*-prise	154	*repro*-duce
35	*hydro*-phane	95	*enter*-tain	155	*sub*-lime
36	*hydro*-phobia	96	*inter*-cept	156	*sub*-mit
37	*hypo*-chondriac	97	*inter*-change	157	*subter*-fuge
38	*hypo*-critical	98	*inter*-est	158	*subter*-ranean
39	*imper*-ative	99	*inter*-fere	159	*sup*-ply
40	*incom*-mode	100	*inter*-lace	160	*sup*-port
41	*incom*-pact	101	*inter*-leave	161	*super*-add
42	*incom*-petent	102	*inter*-line	162	*super*-cargo
43	*incon*-stant	103	*inter*-link	163	*super*-fine
44	*incor*-poral	104	*inter*-lope	164	*super*-lative
45	*com*-bine	105	*inter*-lude	165	*temp*-er
46	*com*-port	106	*inter*-marriage	166	*temp*-oral
47	*com*-merce	107	*inter*-meddle	167	*tran*-quil
48	*com*-mit	108	*inter*-mingle	168	*tran*-scend
49	*com*-mune	109	*inter*-mit	169	*trans*-fer
50	*com*-pact	110	*inter*-mix	170	*trans*-fix
51	*com*-pany	111	*inter*-pose	171	*trans*-fuse
52	*com*-pass	112	*inter*-sect	172	*trans*-gress
53	*com*-pel	113	*inter*-val	173	*trans*-late
54	*com*-ply	114	*inter*-vene	174	*trans*-mit
55	*com*-pile	115	*inter*-view	175	*trans*-mute
56	*com*-pose	116	*obsti*-nate	176	*trans*-pire
57	*com*-press	117	*oppor*-tune	177	*trans*-pose
58	*com*-pute	118	*oppro*-brium	178	*exer*-cise
59	*con*-cave	119	*per*-chance	179	*extir*-pate
60	*con*-ceal	120	*per*-mit	180	*expli*-cate

EXERCISE XXIV.

#		#		#	
1	en-*act*	55	geo-*graphy*	109	great-*ness*
2	ex-*act*	56	steno-*graphy*	110	meek-*ness*
3	bal-*ance*	57	lan-*guish*	111	quick-*ness*
4	deliver-*ance*	58	extin-*guish*	112	wilder-*ness*
5	griev-*ance*	59	ex-*hibit*	113	dis-*plant*
6	guid-*ance*	60	man-*hood*	114	im-*plant*
7	reli-*ance*	61	maiden-*hood*	115	im-*prove*
8	vari-*ance*	62	widow-*hood*	116	re-*quest*
9	ten-*ant*	63	ed-*ify*	117	ac-*quit*
10	a-*ble*	64	test-*ify*	118	democ-*racy*
11	bab-*ble*	65	grav-*ity*	119	cata-*ract*
12	bi-*ble*	66	real-*ity*	120	cor-*rect*
13	capa-*ble*	67	sincer-*ity*	121	e-*rect*
14	dura-*ble*	68	prosper-*ity*	122	di-*rect*
15	ena-*ble*	69	van-*ity*	123	in-*scribe*
16	fee-*ble*	70	re-*ject*	124	forti-*tude*
17	gam-*ble*	71	en-*join*	125	grati-*tude*
18	no-*ble*	72	de-*claim*	126	lati-*tude*
19	porta-*ble*	73	re-*cline*	127	recti-*tude*
20	ta-*ble*	74	in-*clude*	128	desti-*tute*
21	tum-*ble*	75	dis-*count*	129	prosti-*tute*
22	trem-*ble*	76	man-*ly*	130	dis-*tinct*
23	visi-*ble*	77	love-*ly*	131	re-*verse*
24	defen-*dant*	78	low-*ly*	132	di-*vest*
25	ver-*dant*	79	high-*ly*	133	back-*ward*
26	ar-*dent*	80	late-*ly*	134	home-*ward*
27	diffi-*dent*	81	care-*less*	135	in-*ward*
28	de-*duct*	82	rest-*less*	136	out-*ward*
29	exist-*ence*	83	e-*lect*	137	to-*ward*
30	infer-*ence*	84	neg-*lect*	138	east-*ward*
31	rever-*ence*	85	se-*lect*	139	west-*ward*
32	what-*ever*	86	de-*mand*	140	north-*ward*
33	where-*ever*	87	re-*mand*	141	south-*ward*
34	who-*ever*	88	a-*mend*	142	bra-*zier*
35	de-*fect*	89	depart-*ment*	143	gla-*zier*
36	re-*flect*	90	gar-*ment*	144	ho-*sier*
37	in-*flict*	91	pay-*ment*	145	lei-*sure*
38	un-*iform*	92	mo-*ment*	146	mea-*sure*
39	man-*ful*	93	defer-*ment*	147	plea-*sure*
40	mourn-*ful*	94	attain-*ment*	148	trea-*sure*
41	pain-*ful*	95	atone-*ment*	149	a-*zure*
42	beauti-*ful*	96	argu-*ment*	150	sei-*zure*
43	bounti-*ful*	97	refine-*ment*	151	minia-*ture*
44	doubt-*ful*	98	ele-*ment*	152	na-*ture*
45	duti-*ful*	99	tene-*ment*	153	pic-*ture*
46	wil-*ful*	100	tor-*ment*	154	pos-*ture*
47	sin-*ful*	101	judge-*ment*	155	ven-*ture*
48	play-*ful*	102	senti-*ment*	156	cour-*teous*
49	bash-*ful*	103	conso-*nant*	157	righ-*teous*
50	tune-*ful*	104	preg-*nant*	158	volup-*tuous*
51	fra-*grance*	105	rem-*nant*	159	mar-*tial*
52	para-*graph*	106	depo-*nant*	160	par-*tial*
53	tele-*graph*	107	oppo-*nent*	161	an-*cient*
54	bio-*graphy*	108	suste-*nance*	162	pa-*tience*

EXERCISE XXV.

1	abbre-via-*tion*	61	con-*tract*
2	abro-ga-*tion*	62	contro-ver-*sial*
3	abso-lu-*tion*	63	con-ver-*sion*
4	adver-tise-*ment*	64	con-vers-*ant*
5	advo-ca-*tion*	65	con-voca-*tion*
6	discom-mend	66	con-vul-*sion*
7	discom-menda-*ble*	67	magni-fy-*ing*
8	discom-menda-*tion*	68	misin-*form*
9	discom-pos-*ing*	69	misin-*struct*
10	discon-*nect*	70	miscon-struc-*tion*
11	discon-nec-*tion*	71	multi-pres-*ence*
12	discon-sola-*tion*	72	multi-ply-*ing*
13	discon-tent-*ment*	73	multi-plic-*ity*
14	disen-gage-*ment*	74	enter-pris-*ing*
15	affec-*tion*	75	enter-tain-*ing*
16	affec-ta-*tion*	76	enter-tain-*ment*
17	affirm-a-*ble*	77	inter-cep-*tion*
18	aggra-va-*tion*	78	inter-clude
19	aggre-ga-*tion*	79	inter-est-*ing*
20	agree-ing	80	inter-fer-*ence*
21	agree-*ment*	81	inter-fer-*ing*
22	agree-a-*ble*	82	inter-ject
23	hydro-graphical	83	inter-jec-*tion*
24	com-bat-*ant*	84	inter-mis-*sion*
25	com-bin-*ing*	85	inter-po-*sition*
26	com-bina-*tion*	86	inter-sec-*tion*
27	com-fort-*less*	87	inter-ven-*tion*
28	com-mand-*ant*	88	intro-duc-*tion*
29	com-mand-*ment*	89	ob-ject
30	com-mence-*ment*	90	ob-jec-*tion*
31	com-menc-*ing*	91	ob-la-*tion*
32	com-menda-*ble*	92	ob-serva-*tion*
33	com-mis-*sion*	93	ob-serv-*ance*
34	com-mit-*ment*	94	ob-tain-*ment*
35	com-mo-*tion*	95	oppor-tune-*ly*
36	com-part-*ment*	96	per-cep-*tion*
37	com-pas-*sion*	97	per-di-*tion*
38	com-peti-*tion*	98	per-fec-*tion*
39	com-ply-*ing*	99	per-form-*ance*
40	com-pass-*ing*	100	per-ma-*nent*
41	com-po-*sition*	101	per-mis-*sion*
42	com-pres-*sion*	102	per-va-*sion*
43	com-pul-*sion*	103	pre-cau-*tion*
44	con-cep-*tion*	104	pre-fer-*ment*
45	con-ces-*sion*	105	pre-fix-*ing*
46	con-coc-*tion*	106	pre-hen-*sion*
47	con-demn-*ing*	107	pre-sump-*tion*
48	con-di-*tion*	108	pre-tend-*ing*
49	con-fer-*ence*	109	pre-ten-*sion*
50	con-ferr-*ing*	110	pre-vail-*ing*
51	con-fes-*sion*	111	pre-ven-*tion*
52	con-fine-*ment*	112	pro-ba-*tion*
53	con-fu-*sion*	113	pro-ces-*sion*
54	con-*nect*	114	pro-crastina-*tion*
55	con-nec-*tion*	115	pro-cura-*tion*
56	con-sign-*ment*	116	pro-cur-*ing*
57	con-sola-*tion*	117	pro-duc-*ing*
58	con-sump-*tion*	118	pro-fan-*ing*
59	con-tempti-*ble*	119	pro-fess-*ing*
60	con-tent-*ment*	120	pro-fes-*sion*

EXERCISE XXV. Continued.

121	pro–gress–*ing*	146	*tempt*–a–*tion*
122	pro–*hibit*	147	*tran*–quill–*ity*
123	pro–*ject*	148	*trans*–*act*
124	pro–tec–*tion*	149	*trans*–fera–*ble*
125	pro–vin–*cial*	150	*trans*–ferr–*ing*
126	pro–vok–*ing*	151	*trans*–figura–*tion*
127	pur–vey–*ance*	152	*trans*–*form*
128	*recom*–menda–*ble*	153	*trans*–form–*ing*
129	*recom*–menda–*tion*	154	*trans*–fusi–*ble*
130	*recom*–mis–*sion*	155	*trans*–fu–*sion*
131	*recom*–mit–*ment*	156	*trans*–gress–*ing*
132	*recom*–po–*sition*	157	*trans*–gres–*sion*
133	*recon*–*duct*	158	*tran*–*sient*
134	*recon*–ver–*sion*	159	*trans*–la–*tion*
135	*recon*–vey–*ance*	160	*trans*–loca–*tion*
136	*recon*–vey–*ing*	161	*trans*–mis–*sion*
137	*repre*–hen–*sion*	162	*trans*–muta–*tion*
138	*repre*–senta–*tion*	163	*trans*–par–*ent*
139	*sub*–mis–*sion*	164	*trans*–*plant*
140	*sub*–*tract*	165	*trans*–planta–*tion*
141	*sub*–trac–*tion*	166	*trans*–porta–*tion*
142	*super*–excell–*ence*	167	*trans*–posi–*tion*
143	*super*–impo–*sition*	168	*exer*–*tion*
144	*temp*–er–*ance*	169	*expli*–ca–*ble*
145	*temp*–era–*ment*	170	*expli*–ca–*tion*

ABBREVIATION OF WORDS, ETC.

Many words which do not come under the preceding rule of *Prefixes* and *Terminations*, admit of being expressed by their leading sound or sounds; in such cases, a mark thus ′ should be inserted beneath, to denote the same. Ex. ⌐ *p-q—*, for *pecu-liar, peculiarly,* and *pecu-liarity;* ⌐ *x-km—*, for *excom-municate* and *excommunication, &c.*

EXERCISE XXVI.

1	excom—	excommunicate,-d, excommunication.
2	extem—	extemporary, extemporaneous, extemporise.
3	intem—	intemperate,-ly, intemperance.
4	integ—	integrity.
5	intel—	intellective, intellectual,-ly.
6	intelli—	intelligence, intelligent,-ly.
7	neg—	negligence, negligent,-ly.
8	benev—	benevolence, benevolent,-ly.
9	magnif—	magnificence, magnificent,-ly.
10	magnan—	magnanimous,-ly.
11	manufac—	manufacture,-d,-r,-ing, manufactory.
12	delib—	deliberate,-d,-ly, deliberation.
13	degen—	degeneracy, degenerate,-ness, degeneration.
14	remem—	remember,-ed,-ing, remembrance,-r.
15	remon—	remonstrate, remonstrance, remonstrant.
16	licen—	licentiously, licentiousness.
17	repub—	republic,-an, republicanism, republicanise,-d.
18	stig—	stigma,-tic,-al,-ally, stigmatise,-d.
19	system—	systematic,-al,-ally, systemize,-d,-r,-ing.
20	know—	knowledge.

COMBINATION OF WORDS, ETC.

Although the characters of the Short-Hand alphabet, when standing alone, have been assigned to represent particular words, yet in order to abbreviate and facilitate combination as much as possible, a little variation has been adopted, as exhibited in the following exercise.

EXERCISE XXVII.

1	Let me be.
2	Let me do.
3	Let me have.
4	Let us be.
5	Let us do.
6	Let us have.
7	Let her be.
8	Let her do.
9	Let her have.
10	Let him be.
11	Let him do.
12	Let him have.
13	Let them be.
14	Let them do.
15	Let them have.

When joined together, will express

EXERCISE XXVII. Continued.

16	? ⌒ ⌣	I have had.
17	? ⌣ ⌣	I had had.
18	? ෆ ⌒	I can have.
19	? ℯ ⌒	I could have.
20	? ⌒ ⌒	I may have.
21	? ∕ ⌒	I shall have.
22	? ∖ ⌒	I should have.
23	? ෆ ⌒	I will have.
24	? ℮ ⌒	I would have.
25	⌣ ⌒ ∕	He has done.
26	⌒ ⌣ ∕	He had done.
27	⌒ ⌒ ∕	He may do.
28	⌒ ෆ ∕	He can do.
29	⌣ ℯ ∕	He could do.
30	⌒ ∕ ∕	He shall do.
31	⌣ ∖ ∕	He should do.
32	⌒ ෆ ∕	He will do.
33	⌣ ℮ ∕	He would do.
34	℮ ⌒ ⊂	We have been.
35	ෆ ⌣ ⊂	We had been.
36	ෆ ෆ ⊂	We can be.
37	℮ ℯ ⊂	We could be.
38	ෆ ∕ ⊂	We shall be.
39	℮ ∖ ⊂	We should be.
40	ෆ ෆ ⊂	We will be.
41	℮ ℮ ⊂	We would be.

When joined together, will express

EXERCISE XXVII. Continued.

42	𝓎	/	⌣	(		I shall not be.
43	⌒	ഗ	⌣	/		He can not do.
44	ჿ	⌒	⌣	⌒		We will not have.
45	∪	ഋ	⌒	(		He could have been.
46	∪	ഋ	⌒	/		He could have done.
47	∪	ഋ	⌒	∪		He could have had.
48	ℓ	ഋ	⌒	(		We could have been.
49	ℓ	ഋ	⌒	/		We could have done.
50	ℓ	ഋ	⌒	∪		We could have had.
51	—	ഋ	⌒	(		They could have been.
52	—	ഋ	⌒	/		They could have done.
53	—	ഋ	⌒	∪		They could have had.
54	∪	ℓ	⌒	(		He would have been.
55	ℓ	ℓ	⌒	/		We would have done.
56	—	ℓ	⌒	∪		They would have had.
57	𝓎	٩	—	(		I ought to be.
58	𝓎	٩	—	/		I ought to do.
59	𝓎	٩	—	⌒		I ought to have.
60	∪	ρ	—	(		He ought to be.
61	∪	ρ	—	/		He ought to do.
62	∪	ρ	—	⌒		He ought to have.
63	ℓ	ρ	—	(		We ought to be.
64	ℓ	ρ	—	/		We ought to do.
65	ℓ	ρ	—	⌒		We ought to have.
66	—	ρ	—	(		They ought to be.
67	—	ρ	—	/		They ought to do.
68	—	ρ	—	⌒		They ought to have.

When joined together, will express

NATURAL CONTRACTIONS.

1	*a*	Alone.
2	@	About.
3	@	Around.
4	○	World, the world.
5	⊕	Through the world.
6	⊙	High, or up in the world.
7	⊙	Low, or down in the world.
8	○	Upon the world.
9	-○	Coming into the world.
10	○-	Going out of the world.
11	○○	Before the world.
12	○○	After the world.
13	⊙	In the world.
14	○	The beginning of the world.
15	○	The end of the world.
16	θ	Through.
17	+′	Christ, Christ's.
18	+	Christian, christianity.
19	×	Crucify, crucified, crucifixion.
20	ε	Before.
21	ᴖ	Behind.
22	ε	Between, betwixt.
23	=	Equal, equally, equality.
24	=	Unequal, unequally.
25	>	Majority.
26	≤	Minority.
27	⊥	Perpendicular, -ly.

NUMERALS.

Those who prefer Short-Hand marks for numbers, instead of figures, may adopt the following :

1	2	3	4	5	6	7	8	9	0
—	\	/	|	⌒	⌄	⌐	(	)	⌐

always remembering to distinguish them from letters, by placing a dash over them, thus, ⌐ 14 ; ∨ 23 ; ⌐ 41 ; ⌐ 60 ; ⌐ 967 ; ⌐ 8367, &c.

EXERCISE XXVIII.

The Lord will bless them that fear him, both small and-great.* Our help is in the name of the Lord, who made heaven and-earth.* O give thanks unto the God of-gods;† for his mercy endur-*eth* for ever. I will yet praise thee more and-more.† I will extol thee my God, O King; and I will bless thy name for ever and-ever.† Every day will I bless thee; and I will praise thy name for ever and-ever.+

* See Words of contrary signification, p. 78.
† See Repetition of Words and Sentences, p. 76.

For thou, O Lord, art high above all the earth ; thou art exalted far above all gods. Let-them-praise-the name of the Lord; for his name ALONE* is excellent, his glory is above the earth and-heaven. Praise ye the Lord. Praise-ye-the-Lord from the heavens ; praise him in the heights. This God is our God for ever and-ever; he-will-be our guide, even unto death. Peace, peace, to him that is far off, and to him that is near, saith the Lord, and I-will heal him. *Com*-fort ye, comfort-ye, my people, saith your God.

EXERCISE XXIX.

TERMINATIONS PRINTED IN *ITALICS*.

Thou hast been my help, leave me not, neither forsake me, O God of my salva-*tion*. Let thy mercy, O Lord, be upon us, accord-*ing* as we hope in thee. Cast-*ing* all your care upon Him, for he car-*eth* for you. The Lord is my strength and song, and he is become my salva-*tion*. God be merci-*ful* to me a sinner. In whom we-have redemp-*tion* THROUGH* his blood, even the forgive-*ness* of

See Natural Contractions, page 95.

E

sins. He that trust-*eth* in his own heart is
a fool. Give us help from trou-*ble*, for vain
is the help of man. The Lord is merci-*ful*
and gra-*cious*, slow to anger, and plente-*ous*
in mercy. The Lord will be a refuge for
the oppressed, a refuge in times of trou-*ble*.
The meek will he guide in judge-*ment*, and
the meek will he teach his way. Serve the
Lord with glad-*ness*. Hide not thy face
from me in the day when I am in trou-*ble*.
The fear of the Lord is the begin-*ning* of
wisdom. Justice and judge-*ment* are the
habita-*tion* of thy throne, mercy and truth
shall go BEFORE* thy face. The Lord is my
por-*tion*, saith my soul ; therefore will I hope
in him. I-will look unto the Lord, I-will
wait for the God of my salva-*tion*, my God
will hear me. Lord, lift thou up the light of
thy counte-*nance* upon us. I-have waited
for thy salva-*tion*, O Lord. Save us, O God
of our salva-*tion*. Let not your heart be
trou-*bled*, neither let it be afraid. The Lord
is my light and my salva-*tion*, whom shall I
fear ? Be not faith-*less*, but believ-*ing*. Be
not weary in well do*ing*. God is our refuge

* See page 95.

and strength, a very pres-*ent* help in trou-*ble*. God is my salva-*tion* and my glory; the rock of my strength is in God. Hum-*ble* yourselves in the sight of the Lord, and he-shall lift you up. Be thou faith-*ful* unto death, and I-will give thee a crown of life. Let your modera-*tion* be known unto all men. Let-us-not-be* weary in well do-*ing*. Be merci-*ful* unto me, O Lord, for I cry unto thee dai-*ly*. Though I walk in the midst of trou-*ble*, thou wilt revive me. All the ends of the earth shall see the salva-*tion* of our God. Behold thy salva-*tion* com-*eth*; behold his re-*ward* is with him and his work BEFORE† him. He only is my rock and my salva-*tion*. He giv-*eth* grace unto the low-*ly*. Thou art my refuge and my por-*tion*. Show us thy mercy, O Lord, and grant us thy salva-*tion*. Behold I come quick-*ly*, and my re-*ward* is with me.

* See page 92.　　　† See page 95.

567934

EXERCISE XXX.

PREFIXES AND TERMINATIONS PRINTED IN ITALICS.

Pre-serve me, O God, for in thee do I put my trust. The Lord shall *pre*-serve thee from all evil; he-shall *pre*-serve thy soul. If ye love me, keep my *com*-mand-*ments*. Thou wilt keep in *per-fect* peace, whose mind is stayed on thee. Let your *con*-versa-*tion* be such as it becom-*eth* the gospel of CHRIST.* Know thou the God of thy father, and serve him with a *per-fect* heart, and with a will-*ing* mind. He-will turn again, he-will-have *com*-pas-*sion* upon us. I-will-not leave you *com*-fort-*less*, I-will come to you. If ye keep my *com*-mand-*ments*, ye shall abide in my love. Watch and pray, that ye enter not into *tempt*-a-*tion*. The Lord is gra-*cious* and full of *com*-pas-*sion*, slow to anger and of great mercy. Lead us not into *tempt*-a-*tion*, but deliver us from evil. Let, I pray thee, thy merci-*ful* kind-*ness* be for my com-fort. I-will run the way of thy *com*-mand-*ments*, when thou shalt enlarge my heart. God-*liness* with *con*-tent-*ment* is great gain.

See Natural Contractions, page 95.

Specimen

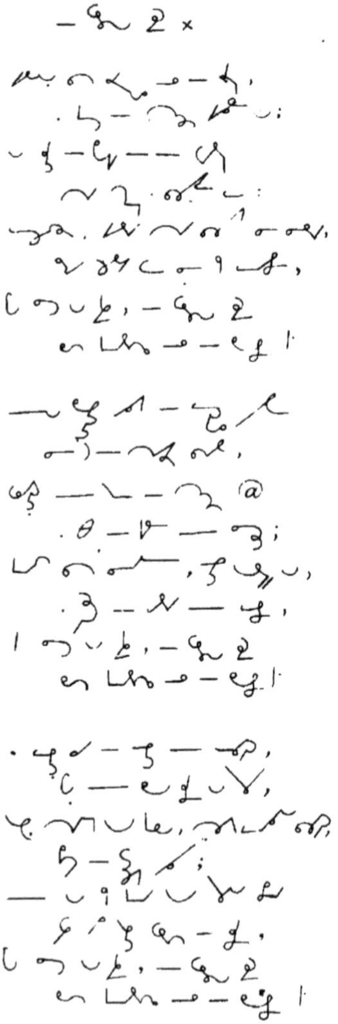

Translation of the Specimen of Short-Hand.

THE BEACON-LIGHT.

Darkness was deepening o'er the seas,
　And still the hulk drove on ;
No sail to answer to the breeze
　Her masts and cordage gone :
Gloomy and drear her course of fear,
　Each look'd but for a grave,
When full in sight, the beacon-light
　Came streaming o'er the wave !

Then wildly rose the gladdening shout
　Of all that hardy crew—
Boldly they put the helm about,
　And through the surf they flew ;
Storm was forgot, toil heeded not,
　And loud the cheer they gave,
As full in sight, the beacon light
　Came streaming o'er the wave !

And gaily oft the tale they told,
　When they were safe on shore,
How hearts had sunk, and hope grown cold,
　Amid the billows' roar ;
That not a star had shone afar
　By its pale beam to save,
When full in sight, the beacon-light
　Came streaming o'er the wave !

FOR THE LEARNER'S PRACTICE.

THE BRIDE.

I saw her on the nuptial day
Ere hymen's knot was tied,
When all were in their best array
And friends with hearts and faces gay
Press'd round to hail the bride ;
She gaily smil'd, yet could I spy
A tear-drop lurking in her eye.
Again when she to him was led
Who that day call'd her his,
Though blithe her look, and light her tread,
And slight the blush that o'er her spread,
Yet I beheld her vainly try
To check the tear that dimm'd her eye.
I saw her at the altar kneel,
And heard the vow ascend,
In joy and pain, and woe and weal,
Mid changing scenes, unchang'd to feel,
To love till life should end ;
She falter'd not, nor heav'd a sigh,
But yet a tear roll'd from her eye.

Say why that sign of sorrow,
Why did grief's emblem start,
Was it by some austere command,
A ruthless joining of the hand
Without the plighted heart?
Or had they sought, and sought in vain
A parent's prayer and kiss to gain?
No, 'twas not thus, for friends approv'd,
And heart and hand were join'd,
But parting thoughts her spirit mov'd
To friends she long and dearly lov'd
She now must leave behind;
To part from home and kindred dear,
'Twas *this* that caus'd the starting tear.
But all thou'st lost, O may'st thou find
In him who claims thy love,
And though thou leavest home behind
And parents dear and kindred kind
Yet may he dearer prove,
And may much bliss to both be given,
And may ye live and love in heaven.

BOYS OF SWITZERLAND.

Our cot was shelter'd by a wood,
And near a lake's green margin stood ;
A mountain bleak behind us frown'd
Whose top the snow in summer crown'd.
But pastures rich, and warm to boot,
Lay smiling at the mountain's foot ;
There first we frolick'd hand in hand
Two infant boys of Switzerland.

When scarcely old enough to know
The meaning of a tale of wo,
'Twas then by mother we were told
That father in his grave lay cold :
That livelihoods were hard to get
And we too young to labour yet ;
And tears within her eyes would stand
For her two boys of Switzerland.

But soon for mother as we grew,
We work'd as much as boys could do,
Our daily gains to her we bore,
But, ah ! she'll ne'er receive them more ;
For long we watch'd beside her bed,
Then sobb'd to see her lay there dead ;
And now we wander hand in hand,
Two orphan boys of Switzerland.

TO ———.

I knew not that I lov'd thee
  Till thou wert far away !
Ah ! 'twas passion's power that mov'd me,
  I knew not half its sway.

I knew thy voice made sweetest
  Of music to my ear ;
I knew the hours fled fleetest,
  Sweet maid, when thou wert near.

I hail'd the streaks that flush'd the morning,
  That beckon'd thee to rise ;
I check'd the envious night's dull awning
  That hid thee from mine eyes.

The dead of night, my slumbers breaking,
  Thy form was ever nigh ;
I thought of thee asleep or waking,
  Yet, ah ! I knew not why.

No fever'd flush betray'd my feeling,
  My heart was blithe and free ;
I knew not that the flame was stealing,
  Kindled, dear maid, for thee.

Still and smooth the tide and pleasure
  That rolls my life along ;
Soft the link that tied my treasure,
  I knew not, oh ! how strong.

I knew not till the light bark bore me
  Unto the far off sea,
Then first I knew the pang that tore me,
  The pang of love for thee.

Oh ! who could sit and see thee smile,
  Nor smile in turn with thee ?
Who see thine eye with bright tears filling
  Nor weep responsively ?

Who mingle smiles, and mingle weeping,
  Soon feel their spirits one ;
For what is love, but the heart-strings keeping
  In deep felt unison ?

Affections, like the conscience, are rather
to be led than drawn ; and it is to be feared,
they that marry where they do not love,
will love where they do not marry.

TO ————

I wish, but oh ! I dare not say
   The warmest wish I feel for thee ;
I wish thine hours may flout as gay
   As sunbeams on the dark blue sea.

I need not ask thy form more fair,
   Thine eye more full of sympathy,
Thine own sweet smile that lingers there
   Forbids that heedless wish for thee.

I only ask for brighter years,
   A bosom free from sorrow ;
A cheek unbleach'd by dark'ning tears
   A smile for every future morrow.

The way to gain a good reputation is to
endeavour to be what you desire to appear.

Guilt may attain temporal splendour, but
can never confer real happiness.

A FATHER'S SORROW.

I bid thee go in grief and tears, fair daughter of my heart,
For brightest days are clouded oft, and sweetest joys depart ;
Thou'lt find this world so flattering now, alas ! a vale of tears,
The cup of our existence fill'd with sorrow and with fears.

I give thee to thy lover's arms, my beautiful—my child—
For well I know thy guileless heart has fondly on him smil'd ;
He'll take thee to the altar, a young and blooming bride,
But hard I feel it is to part with all a father's pride.

I think me of the days gone by when on thy mother's breast,
I us'd to watch thy infant sleep and bless thy place of rest ;
And often in the even-tide I took thee on my knee,
And happily the hours went on amid thy childhood's glee.

I think me of the loving eye of thy young maidenhood,
When joyfully to greet me home, thou'st by the jasmine stood ;
And all thy gentle words are fresh e'en now upon my ear,
The music of thy youth which us'd a father's heart to cheer.

When thy mother's cheek grew pale and her farewell kiss was given,
And the blessed angel took her to live with God in heaven ;
How oft I twin'd my fingers in thy dark raven hair,
And trac'd her features in thy face, and found a portrait there.

I bid thee go in grief and tears, fair daughter of my heart,
For brightest days are clouded oft, and sweetest joys depart ;
Thou'lt find this world so flattering now, alas ! a vale of tears,
The cup of our existence fill'd with sorrow and with fears.

I hope that he will be to thee, the good—the fond—the true—
And never then thy marriage hour like some thou'lt vainly rue ;
When sorrow's in thy dwelling, love, he'll take thee to his heart,
And kiss away each bitter tear that from thy eyelids start.

He'll bless thee at his going out, and at his coming in,
And thou wilt catch each look of love, and strive e'en more to win;
He will be thy strength in weakness, thy joy in sorrow's hour,
Thy friend before a faithless world, thy rainbow in the shower.

When friends have false or fickle prov'd, and care sits on his brow,
When fortune's lash is keenly felt, remember then thy vow;
And take him in his sadden'd mood, thy fairy hands caress,
And let him know the treasure which in thee he does possess.

Thou'lt thus be round him all thy days, a tender graceful flower,
And he will be thy safe-guard from the ruthless tempest's power;
Close clasp thy love together, be his beauty and his pride,
And the "shadow of a rock" be thine throughout the desert wide.

I bless thee then my gentle girl, receive my benison,
And may the tie now nearly wove, be form'd again in heaven;
And though in bidding thee farewell, there's sadness on my brow,
I'll lead thee to the altar, God's blessing on thy vow.

---

*Concluding sentence of the Speech of the Right Honourable
Lord Brougham, Lord High Chancellor of England, on the
Second Reading of the Reform Bill. Delivered in the House
of Lords, on Friday, the 7th of October, 1831.*

THIS I know, that as sure as man is man,
the delay of justice serves but to enhance the
price at which you must purchase safety
and peace. Your Lordships are the highest
judicial authority in the realm; you sit
here as judges in all causes, civil and crimi-
nal, which can come between subject and

subject. It is the first office of judges, never to decide in any, the most trifling cause, without hearing every thing that can be given in evidence concerning it. Will you decide the great cause of a nation's hopes and fears without a hearing? Beware of your decision. Rouse not the spirit of a peace-loving, but determined people, alienate not the affections of a great empire from your body.

As your friend, as the friend of my country, as the servant of my sovereign, I counsel you to assist with all your efforts to preserve the national peace, and perpetuate the national prosperity. For all these reasons, I pray and beseech you not to reject this bill. I call upon you by all that you hold most dear, by all that binds every one of us to our common order and our common country, unless, indeed, you are prepared to say that you will admit of no reform, that you are resolved against all change, for in that case, opposition would at least be consistent; I beseech you, I solemnly adjure you, yea, even on bended knees, my lords, I implore you not to reject this bill.

NINE USEFUL REMARKS.—1. Hear much and speak little; for the Tongue is the instrument of the greatest good and greatest evil that is in the world.

2. Forget not in thy youth to be mindful of thy end; for though the old man cannot live long, yet the young man may die quickly.

3. Education and instruction are the means; the one by use, the other by precept, to make our natural faculty of reason both the better and the sooner to judge rightly between truth and error, good and evil.

4. A mind well turned and long exercised in virtue, does not easily change any course it once undertakes.

5. Let not the blessings we daily receive from God, make us not to value, or not praise him because they are common.

6. It is impossible to make people understand their ignorance; for it requires knowledge to perceive it; and, therefore, he that can perceive it hath it not.

7. Nothing is truly infamous but what is truly wicked; and, therefore shame can never disturb an innocent and virtuous mind.

8. He who lies under the dominion of any one vice, must expect the common effects of it; if lazy, to be poor; if intemperate, to be diseased; if luxurious, to die betimes.

9. A wise man wants but little, because he desires not much.

The following extracts have been copied from an interesting work entitled "The Young Man's Own Book, A Manual of Intellectual Improvement," recently published by Thos. Tegg and Son, London; price 3s. 6d.

VALUE OF TIME.—Above all things, learn to put a due value on time, and husband every moment as if it were to be your last. You should dispose of the time past to observation and reflection, of the time present to duty, and of the time to come to Providence. In time is comprehended all we possess, enjoy, or wish for; and in losing that, we lose them all. This is a lesson that can never be too often or too earnestly inculcated, es-

pecially to young people; for they are apt
to flatter themselves, they have a large stock
upon their hands, and that, though days,
months, and years, are wantonly wasted,
they are still rich in the remainder. But,
alas! no mistake can be greater, or more
fatal. The moments thus prodigally confounded, are the most valuable that time
distils from his alembic; they partake of the
highest flavour, and breathe out the richest
odour; and as on one hand, they are irre-
trievable, so neither, on the other, can all
the artifice of more experienced life compen-
sate these losses.

ESTEEM AND AFFECTION.—Endeavour by
every proper means to cultivate the esteem
and affection of all; study to be obliging;
this is not only a most amiable, but a most
profitable disposition; do not be too familiar
with any persons, and at the same time be
not too distant; both of these qualities produce contempt: pray much to God; and
neglect no opportunity of cultivating your
mind.   DR. ADAM CLARKE.

NECESSITY OF HAVING FIXED PRINCI-
PLES.—The surest guarantee of success in
every great and laudable enterprise, is decision of character; and no one ever attained
this enviable characteristic without acquiring
the habit of acting upon fixed principles.

In all arts and sciences there are certain
fixed principles, which must be known and
carefully attended to, if a man wishes to
be successful. A mechanic sometimes, by
mere dint of habit and knack, becomes very
expert; but it is only in some confined instance. Just in that track he proceeds with
certainty, but cannot attempt any thing else,
nor even aim at improvement in what he
does. Nay, if he does not understand the
principles on which his operations depend,
he must sometimes fail: he is confounded
by any new appearance, and knows not how
to obviate the least difficulty. But if his
knowledge precedes his activity, if he under-
stands why things must so be done, and how
the effect is produced, he becomes more

adroit in his operations : he can remedy any mistake, can rectify any imperfection, can venture even beyond his accustomed limits, to improvement or new inventions.

Surely then, the art of living honourably, and filling in a respectable manner our station in life, must not be left to hazard, to habit, to custom, to chance, to caprice. He who would be successful and adroit, has need to well understand what rules may guide him : else he may weary himself to no purpose, and fail even by excess of exertion.

Does a youth take up the noble resolution, and determine to be a valuable character, good at least, and great if circumstances permit ; he has made the first step by such a resolution. Let him carefully examine by what principles he may guide himself, to secure so important an object. Let him be assured, that nothing really valuable will be obtained without care and labour. Chance, as it is called, is indolence in this case, and will certainly produce mischief.

A little thinking will show, that men of

any character, good or bad, do act thus on a sort of regular plan.

Some general principle, for instance, suffices in many cases. "That honesty is the best policy," has become a proverb; and it has kept many a one from ruin. There are indeed meaner spirits, who cannot form an idea of policy without craft and subtlety; this soon becomes deceit; and when it sinks to this, it is discovered, and defeats its own purpose. Let the youth then exert a little observation, see what general principles conduct to respectability; and let him select such as have been well tried, such as may peculiarly suit his own situation; to guide him in specific difficulties, or to guard him against his peculiar temptations. The very determination to act on principle will lead to his adopting, one after another, such as more appropriately suit his exigencies. How ought I to act? will become a continual inquiry; and the answer will seldom be very difficult to ascertain, when the custom of discrimination is once thoroughly established.

MEMORY.—A ready recollection of our knowledge, at the moment when we have occasion for it, is a talent of the greatest importance. The man possessed of it seldom fails to distinguish himself in whatever sort of business he may be engaged. It is indeed evident that where the power of retention is weak, all attempts at eminence of knowledge must be vain : for memory is a primary and fundamental power, without which there could be little other intellectual operation. Judgement and reasoning suppose something already known, and draw their decisions only from experience. Imagination selects ideas from the treasures of remembrance, and produces novelty only by varied combinations. We do not even form conjectures of distant, or anticipations of future events, but by concluding what is possible from what is past.

MEANS OF IMPROVING THE MEMORY.—
Of a faculty so important as memory, many
rules have been given for the regulation
and improvement; of which, the first is,
that he who wishes to have a clear and distinct remembrance, should be temperate with
respect to eating, drinking, and sleeping.
The memory depends very much on the state
of the brain, and therefore whatever is hurt-
ful to the latter, must be prejudicial to the
former.   Too much sleep clouds the brain,
and too little overheats it; therefore either
of these extremes must of course injure the
memory, and ought carefully to be avoided.
Intemperance of all kinds, and excess of passion, have the same ill effects; so that we
rarely meet with an intemperate person
whose memory is at once clear and tenacious.
   The art of memory is little more than the
art of *attention*.   What we wish to remember, we should attend to, so as to understand
it perfectly, fixing our view particularly upon
its importance or singular nature.   We
should disengage our minds from all other

things, that we may attend more effectually to the object which we wish to remember. No man can read with much advantage who is not able at pleasure to evacuate his mind, or who brings not to his author an intellect neither turbid with care, nor agitated with pleasure. If the repositories of thought are full, what can they receive? If the mind be employed on the past or the future, the page will be held before the eyes in vain. * * * *

THINKING, not growth, makes manhood. There are some, who, though they have done growing, are still only boys. The constitution may be fixed, while the judgement is immature; the limbs may be strong, while the reasoning is feeble. Many who can run, and jump, and bear any fatigue, cannot observe, cannot examine, cannot reason or judge, contrive, or execute—they do not think.

Accustom yourself then to thinking. Set yourself to understand whatever you see or read. To run through a book is not a dif-

ficult task, nor is it a very profitable one.
To understand a few pages only, is far better than to read the whole, where mere
reading it is all. If the work does not set
you to thinking, either you or the author
must be very deficient.

FINIS.

Henry Mozley and Sons, Printers, Derby.

135

135

135